The
TWILIGHT
of the
PRESIDENCY
From Johnson to Reagan

The
TWILIGHT
of the
PRESIDENCY
From Johnson to Reagan

George E. Reedy, 1917-

Revised Edition

NAL BOOKS

NEW AMERICAN LIBRARY

NEW YORK AND SCARBOROUGH, ONTARIO

Copyright © 1970, 1987 by George E. Reedy

Published simultaneously in Canada
by The New American Library of Canada Limited

NAL TRADEMARK REG. U.S. PAT. OFF. AND FOREIGN COUNTRIES
REGISTERED TRADEMARK—MARCA REGISTRADA
HECHO EN CHICAGO, U.S.A.

SIGNET, SIGNET CLASSIC, MENTOR, ONYX, PLUME, MERIDIAN and
NAL BOOKS are published *in the United States* by NAL PENGUIN INC.,
1633 Broadway, New York, New York 10019,
in Canada by The New American Library of Canada Limited,
81 Mack Avenue, Scarborough, Ontario M1L 1M8

Library of Congress Cataloging-in-Publication Data

Reedy, George E., 1917–
The twilight of the presidency.
Includes index.
1. Presidents—United States. I. Title.
JK516.R35 1987   353.03′1   87-5649
ISBN 0-453-00567-5

Designed by Fritz Metsch

First Printing, September, 1987

1 2 3 4 5 6 7 8 9

PRINTED IN THE UNITED STATES OF AMERICA

Contents

The
TWILIGHT
of the
PRESIDENCY

From Johnson to Reagan

Chapter I

The Flowering of the Presidency

THE OUTSTANDING FEATURE of the twentieth-century evolution of American political institutions has been the emergence of the presidency as the center of national life. The name of any White House incumbent in the present era *is* a household word and very small schoolchildren can identify him for you though they may be mystified as to what he does. For intellectuals and academics, scholarly analysis of the office has become a mass production industry and virtually every newspaper issue or network television newscast includes at least a passing reference to the president or the presidency. Even if the president spends a day loafing, the enormous structure which holds our society together will apprise its readers, listeners, and viewers of that fact.

It was not always so. For those who have lived long enough to have some political consciousness from the pre–Franklin Delano Roosevelt era, there will be memories of local politicians who had far greater name identification than the president, even among educated people. Of course, I spent my childhood in Chicago where we had some very colorful politicians—"Big Bill the Builder" Thompson, "Hinky Dink" Kenna, "Bathhouse" John Coughlin, and "Tubbo" Gilbert. They could keep a whole city entertained during the hottest or coldest weather, especially Thompson, who won a mayoralty race on the platform that he would take the first boat to England and punch King George "on the snoot," and Coughlin, who presided every year over a grand ball in the First Ward that was attended by every bootlegger, pimp, and hooker in the city. It was not just their amusement value that made these men so well known. They had a direct bearing on our daily lives; the president did not. In large areas of the city, the difference between living above or below the poverty line was often a question of a citizen's relationship with his precinct captain and ward leader. They were the links to city hall that could make existence tolerable.

In the slums, there was no other link. Being on good terms with "the boys" meant a turkey at Thanksgiving, a load of coal at Christmas, and little slips of paper that were passports to jobs shoveling snow in the winter or taking care of the city parks in the spring and summer. Furthermore, none of this was a question of "charity." It was an honest open transaction in which the favors were repaid by casting the right vote. The boss was regarded as corrupt only when he rounded up drunks, hoboes, and tramps and voted them in platoons at a number of different precincts where they had been registered under names taken off tombstones in the local cemetery.

At higher social and economic levels, the links were not as strong, but they existed. A group of householders, for example, who wanted their street paved or a school modernized would do well to "stand in right" with their ward leader. Small businesses, which were frequently terrorized by phony "unions," found relief by making reasonably substantial contributions to the party war chest. And a citizen who had wrapped his automobile around a lamppost while loaded with rotgut booze encountered remarkably understanding and sympathetic police at the nearby station, and tolerant magistrates the next morning—

provided that he had been on the proper side in the last election.

At the highest levels, where "bossism" and "machine politics" were openly deplored at every opportunity, there were still some connections, albeit under the table. The police always knew which side of a strike was the "right side" because their intelligence could be keenly honed by the city's political leaders. This was one stratum of society that had some knowledge of the people in Washington. After all, there were federal contracts, not as juicy or plentiful as those in the present economic pool, but nonetheless worthy of consideration.

In the few rural areas with which I was familiar (mostly Michigan and Indiana), mayors were unimportant, and aldermen, ward leaders, and precinct captains did not exist. But my farming relatives and all their friends could recite the names of their representative in the House (usually unknown in the city), their county sheriff, their county judge, and whatever official ran the county school system. The representative was in their minds because he sent them seed samples and useful pamphlets from the Agriculture Department. The place of the others in their hearts was obvious. From later experiences, I suspect that this pattern of bucolic politics which surrounded Newaygo, Michigan, was repeated throughout the nation.

A few presidents were well known—for highly special reasons. Of course we knew about George Washington and Thomas Jefferson (the latter to a lesser extent) because they were "Founding Fathers"—a phrase which called for some form of obeisance just short of genuflection. We knew about Jackson (although we were uncertain whether it was Andrew or Stonewall) because he had fought Indians in Georgia and Florida. We knew about Lincoln and Wilson, because they were war presidents and because we got out of school on Lincoln's birthday. We knew about Teddy Roosevelt because he had led the charge up San Juan Hill and because we all had teddy bears as infants. All other presidents, including the incumbent at any given moment, were anonymous. The extent of this anonymity is amazing in retrospect. As the son of a Chicago newspaperman, I was somewhat precocious in my grasp of the political process. I could name not only the mayor of Chicago but all the members of the City Council, the district attorney, and the county sheriff (both political jobs), as well as an astonishingly large number of ward committeemen and precinct captains. I could even tell you the name of the chairman of the Sanitary District (regarded as a center of boodlery). But I did not have the faintest idea who was our representative in Washington. (I did know the name of one of the senators—James Hamilton Lewis—because my mother had worked in a residential hotel where he lived.) But as for the president, I could name him only because my father took us on a summer vacation to Washington, D.C., and during our tour of the White House my mother was charmed by a portrait of Grace Coolidge. When I asked who she was, I was informed that she was the wife of the president of the United States. That piece of information made me the only child in the neighborhood who could identify the president—and few of my classmates really cared.

During political campaigns people could usually identify the candidates because the names were drilled into their skulls by Republican and Democratic machine leaders who wanted no ticket splitting. But it was not lasting knowledge. The press did not reinforce it with daily communiqués, as the chief executive of the nation—outside of wartime—did little or nothing to justify such communiqués. Because of my father's profession, I was a newspaper reader at a tender age, and I have a very sharp memory. Nevertheless, from the entire Coolidge era, my only newspaper recollections are one picture of him on an Indian reservation posing uneasily in a feathered headdress so large it made his narrow features look as though they were pushed through a cardboard cutout at an amusement park, and one headline announcing that he did not choose to run in 1928.

The press spent very little time covering presidents. When I first came to Washington as a reporter in 1938, there were still some working pre–World War I correspondents. They could recall the days when they were not even allowed inside the White House except when the president planned a speech. On the few occasions that something was in the wind they assembled at the gates on Pennsylvania Avenue and sought interviews with people entering and leaving. Theodore Roosevelt had a few "pets" who were favored with frequent interviews and choice morsels of news. But their positions depended on their "good faith" in writing stories the way Teddy wanted them written and withholding from the public whatever he wanted withheld. Woodrow Wilson, after abandoning a brief attempt to set up press conferences, maintained a form of liaison with the press through a secretary.

What may be even more significant is the virtually total lack of intellectual interest in the presidency in the years that preceded Franklin Roosevelt. The American experiment in government and society was the subject of considerable interest to such nineteenth-century writers as Lord Bryce and Alexis de Tocqueville, but they did not see very much that was remarkable in the office of president as such. Lord Bryce described the chief executive as "an enlarged copy of the State Governor" and "a reduced and improved copy of the British King." He added that "great men are not chosen Presidents." De Tocqueville recognized some of the unique qualities of the office and was prescient in pointing out that presidential powers were "enhanced" by increasing American involvement in foreign affairs. He did not, however, devote any great space to the White House in his monumental *Democracy in America.*

During the Hoover-Smith campaign in 1928, everyone knew the names of the candidates because of a wave of religious bigotry that was sweeping the country. Even children in schoolyards disputed vigorously whether Al Smith's election would mean "a nigger cardinal" to run the United States (an underground whispering charge put in circulation by the Ku Klux Klan). The mood was ugly— but it disappeared the day after the election. The name Herbert Clark Hoover immediately began to fade from the public consciousness as had the names of most of his predecessors. He was not a colorful man and those things in which he was really interested—such as adequate industrial standards—were not the kind of causes that set people to marching in the streets.

Unfortunately for Mr. Hoover, he was the first non–war-connected president whose name was to become a household word. The collapse of the stock market and the deep depression that followed were blamed on him. This was a strange phenomenon, which I have never really understood. The "old folks" in my family had been through depressions and my mother's people were steel-mill workers who usually suffered the most when unemployment began to rise. Not one time, however, had I heard any of them blame the president in office for the very real suffering they had experienced in the past. This changed with Hoover.

The hatred that welled up against Hoover approached new heights of the irrational. Part of it was due to his personality. He was incapable of *appearing* to feel any sympathy for the hungry and the homeless, and his statements about the soundness of the nation's economy were positively fatuous. He wore a high, choke collar that made him look as though he were staring over the heads of the common people and he was plumpish—virtually an affront at a time when hundreds and thousands of men and women were getting their only nourishment from bowls of soup passed out in lines on the street. To make things worse, in his last two years a Democratic Congress opposed him at every opportunity.

Americans vied with each other in finding vicious phrases to describe his presumed inactivity and pasting his name on every unpleasant fact of their lives. The shantytowns that sprang up on the outskirts of every city were known as Hoovervilles. When farm prices fell dramatically and a wave of agricultural foreclosures swept the nation, farmers shot and ate woodchucks, which they dubbed "Hoover hogs." A person who had lost his or her job was said to be "Hooverized." Hoover became the butt of every burlesque comedian in America. In one vaudeville skit I can still recall a doctor saying to a patient: "Just last week, I put a new muscle into the thigh of a total paralytic and now he's walking around." The patient replied: "That's nothing, doc. Look what we put in the White House and now we're all walking around." The bitter laughter that greeted this inane remark was a measure of the depth to which the president had fallen.

The outcome of the 1932 election was as predictable as the return of the swallows to Capistrano. The fact that Hoover received 40 percent of the vote was merely a tribute to the persistence of voting patterns in the twenties and thirties. The "swing" states—those that could change between elections—were solidly for FDR. In the political world, it is the results in the swing states, rather than the overall national percentages, that determine whether an election is close or a landslide. The interesting factor, however, is that Hoover did not depart the White House to march into oblivion. His name really *did* become a household word. The bitter hatred persisted and for at least two decades Democratic aspirants for any office found it convenient to run against him, as southern bigots later found it convenient to run against Martin Luther King, Jr. The age of the presidency had arrived and from then on men would be remembered—for their negative as well as their positive qualities.

After half a century, our view of Roosevelt has changed. No one doubts his political skills, nor does anyone deny that he was the right man for the time. But what seemed like a grand design when he was in office now appears to be a scatter-shot approach to the nation's problems—he threw out idea after idea without giving any problem or solution very much thought. It was World War II rather than the New Deal that put an end to the Great Depression, and one of the most important economic measures was the Reconstruction Finance Corporation, which was established by Hoover. FDR was a vindictive man and he loved the game of pitting White House assistants against one another in a furious attempt to get credit for ideas. When all that is said and done, however, the fact remains that he was a master of the crisis, a leader who was superb at the art of massing hordes of people to battle against great odds. His vision of history may have been limited but his vision of power was colossal. He understood the usages of power to manipulate a society. Not until Lyndon B. Johnson came along twenty years later did a president approach his skill in that area.

What this meant was that historic forces had paved the way for a shift in the American people's preoccupation from local to national government—and a man was at hand to do it. The city, county, and state machines had demonstrated their complete impotence to meet the current economic crisis. Private industry had become a wasteland of abandoned plants and idle machinery. Charity promised nothing but an endless future of soup lines and flophouses for the coldest nights. There was no place to look for hope except to the White House. Roosevelt responded with programs and, what was more important, the right rhetoric. In a few months, the theme song of Americans, which had been "Brother, can you spare a dime?" became "Who's afraid of the big, bad wolf?" Confidence had been restored, even though most of the jobs were on "make work" projects such as WPA.

Although no one realized it at the time, something else had happened. The American people were now conditioned to look to Washington for help when they were in trouble. The local political institutions that had served them in the past had fumbled. Even the big city machines, which had regarded the nation's capital merely as a place to send troublemakers to get them out of the way, now looked to Roosevelt to sustain them in power. He responded willingly, to the great distress of the more idealistic young New Dealers, who did not like the association with the political machines of Frank Hague, Tom Pendergast, Ed Crump, and John Kelly.

The New Deal period of the Roosevelt reign really did not last very long. Most of the legislation was enacted during the the first two years, and an astonishing amount of that was passed by Congress in the first hundred days of the initial session under FDR. A few years later the collapse of Roosevelt's "court packing" proposal and the defeat of his efforts to purge conservative Democrats during the 1938 campaign made it clear that the New Deal programs were not overwhelmingly popular. But it made little difference. He was still the president that most people wanted. He easily defeated Wendell Willkie in 1940 and Tom Dewey in 1944 to become the first (and, unless we amend the Constitution again) the only president to serve more than two terms.

A caution may be necessary here. FDR was not universally loved. In fact, he was hated just as deeply as Herbert Hoover, but by many fewer people. After a few years, staunch Democrats who had been associated with him for decades—such as Al Smith and Jim Farley—left his side deeply disillusioned, as did Raymond Moley, one of the fabled "brain trusters." Much of the hatred came from businessmen who considered him a traitor to his class. The *New Yorker* magazine featured cartoons depicting industry moguls assembled in the Union League Club and groaning aloud as they heard his voice over the radio saying "Mah Friends." Small businessmen turned out to be as anti–New Deal as their big brothers. And after the 1932 elections, most newspapers were against him as well. No one questioned his leadership qualifications, but he never commanded the virtually universal affection that attended Eisenhower and Reagan.

There is no doubt, nevertheless, that Mr. Roosevelt was at the helm during a period of historic development in American institutions. His pump-priming economic measures—PWA, NYA, CCC, WPA—are now merely historical curiosities. His regulatory measures—SEC, FAA, FCC*—have become so accepted that few people associate them with his name. It may well be that he will join the ranks of those presidents who owe their immortality solely to a war. But the fact remains that he made the presidency a living reality to Americans and began the period when the White House became the focal point of the nation's social, economic, and political life.

*PWA—Public Works Administration; NYA—National Youth Administration; CCC—Civilian Conservation Corps; WPA—Works Progress Administration; SEC—Securities and Exchange Commission; FAA—Federal Aviation Administration; FCC—Federal Communications Commission.

Chapter II

The American Monarchy

THE ATTENTION PAID to the president and the presidency highlighted a quality of the office that had been there all along but had not been noticed. Essentially, the presidency *is* a form of monarchy, but a form that had not had much of an opportunity to display its true character before Franklin D. Roosevelt and the New Deal. True, there had been occasions on which presidents had taken far-reaching steps paying only scant obeisance to the constitutional requirements. Jefferson purchased the Louisiana Territory without giving Congress an advance opportunity to pass judgment. Andrew Jackson defied the Supreme Court on the issue of states' rights. Abraham Lincoln suspended guarantees of individual freedom, including the writ of habeas corpus. Teddy Roosevelt sent the navy on a trip halfway around the world, contrary to the will of Congress. But these had all been regarded by writers and intellectuals as isolated instances that were justified by unusual and urgent circumstances. The proper conclusion was not drawn from any of them: Within certain limitations, the president *is* the nation, not merely the manager of its affairs.

This is not to say that the president has all the powers once enjoyed by the Bourbons, the Hohenzollerns, the Hapsburgs, and the Romanovs. Power is not the essence of monarchy. One need note only that the most stable

11

throne in the world today belongs to Queen Elizabeth of England, who certainly has less power than any prime minister. The fundamental quality of kingship is the status of the king or queen as the nation itself. In the immortal words of Louis XIV: "L'Etat c'est moi." In a truly divided power system (and ours is that despite the skeptics) no president can be as willful in the exercise of his office as Louis XIV. The American king must get money from Congress; he must abide by the decisions of the courts; he must face the electorate or leave the White House in four years. He can, however, be arbitrary within the constitutional sphere allotted to him, and he possesses a power of initiative (discussed at length later) that enables him to invade the domain of the other branches of government. What may be most important is that he can set the goals for the nation during his term of office. Both Congress and the courts can make his pursuit of those goals a futile endeavor, but they cannot set substitute goals, and they can try to impose their visions of the future on the president only by resorting to his removal by procedures that are catastrophic.

The simple point is that when we speak of leadership of or by the United States we mean *presidential* leadership. When we speak of the policy of the United States we mean the *president's* policy. And when we say that the United States is acting in any manner, we mean that the *president* is acting. From the practical standpoint of what happens by design in world affairs, the terms president and United States are synonymous. There is nothing similar in the political structure of any parliamentary democracy, where a prime minister must get a cabinet consensus for every action he or she proposes. That would be a very strange world to an American chief executive who discovers after a few months in the White House that he can ignore his cabinet officers in setting goals and can then direct those same people to use their agencies to carry out programs regardless of the feelings of the agency heads. What could be more monarchical? There is an important corollary to the situation: The president really has two jobs. The one that has received the most attention is that of his managerial role, his (probably "her" before very long) responsibility for handling the nation's affairs. Coupled with that is his role of personifying the nation and becoming thereby the unifying factor that holds us together. No prime minister holds such a position—although Josef Stalin exuded a czarlike aura during his lifetime. It is only in South America and the Philippines—nations that modeled their constitutions after ours—that anything similar can be found. (Unfortunately, those nations omitted to place teeth in the checks and balances that keep an American president from going completely overboard, and the result is the constant specter of revolution as the only way of getting rid of a dictator.) It is this dual role that makes the presidency so fascinating intellectually. It has produced a body of political science literature that has no parallel in other governmental fields or in studies of other governments. By comparison, the volumes and monographs on prime ministers and constitutional monarchs seem to be positively anemic. Those which do exist usually consider the positions as easily understandable elements of political systems rather than unique institutions. Most scholars would agree with that assumption.

Many problems arise out of assigning double duty to the president, and all of them flow from the fact that the two roles are mutually exclusive. To sustain his position as a symbol of unity the president should keep strictly out of politics and out of management of the government. Even favors to people can be deadly (the Greeks noted that every favor conferred upon anyone results in nineteen enemies and one ingrate). To manage the affairs of government, the president must decide between competing claimants for social and economic advantage. Such decisions cannot be made without dividing people and creating enmities, which blotches the unifying symbols. An astute president can walk a tightrope for a considerable period of time, but in the end, he cannot win for losing.

Another problem lies in the tendency of the unifying aspects of the office to separate a man from the political realities of his times. The president may not have the powers of a monarch, but he is treated like one in his personal life. This was not always the case. There was a time when President Adams could go skinny-dipping in the Potomac, and Andrew Jackson's inauguration party turned into a brawl which left drunks in muddy boots sleeping on the White House furniture. There was a period when chief executives could emulate Harun ar-Rashid and wander alone at night to learn what people were really thinking. If any one of them tried it today, he would be leading troops of Secret Service agents through the streets of Washington and would be about as inconspicuous as a whale in the Reflecting Pool below the Lincoln Memorial.

Over the past half century, the isolation of the president from the lives of the people has grown with each administration. There are a number of reasons for this development. To some extent, it is a function of the president's increased vulnerability to assassination. His security guards would prefer to keep him from physical contact—or even proximity—to anyone. When he proceeds through cities it is in a vehicle that, for all practical purposes, is a small tank in a shell that makes it look like a limousine. To me, it is symbolically significant that when they had finished building the vehicle, they discovered that it totally excluded all sounds from the outside. Therefore, they built in some electronic equipment that permits the occupants of the car to hear the crowd sounds pumped in through radio. One more physical contact between the president and the people is now indirect.

There are other, more potent factors fostering presidential isolation. One of them is the demise of the nation's political parties as election mechanisms. Franklin Roosevelt and Harry Truman had to pay considerable attention to local party leaders because they could withhold or deliver crucial votes. At the same time, those party bosses were close to their constituents and did not hesitate to let presidents know how the people felt. Even FDR had to yield to the bosses who didn't want Henry Wallace to be his vice president for a second term. Today the political parties are, at most, coalition nominating mechanisms that presidential candidates shove into the nearest closet as soon as the national conventions have made their choices.

Part of the problem grows out of the massive character of most of the issues of modern times. We live in a mass society that can be controlled only by impersonal means. We are forced to rely on computers, statistical analysis, and the reduction of human problems to units that can be quantified and manipulated by machines. It is little wonder that the man at the top of the structure finds reality in long sheets of ruled paper crowded with numbers rather than in faces crowded with apprehension or determination. Furthermore, most presidential communications with the American people are through television or radio—two media that reduce communication to a one-way street.

The most important factor, however, is simply the massive character of American government itself. Like it or not, the management of our affairs is now in the hands of a huge machine that is only partially responsive to the people and that obeys inner laws of its own construction. We are accustomed to a system in which attainment of our national desires was conditioned only on the availability of natural resources and the creation of a sufficiently sizable majority to order their use. But a new factor has entered the picture. In addition to the physical resources and a popular consensus, it is now necessary to cope with a sluggish, bureaucratic mass that has a motion and a will of its own. We are learning the realities of the situation the hard way as Congress struggles to balance the budget.

Newton's first law holds that a body at rest will remain at rest and a body in motion will continue in motion along the same line until acted on by an outside force. The federal bureaucracy is like that. It can be moved by a determined president. But once the motion has started and the course has been set, the internal momentum of our government's machinery continues with the implacable determination of an advancing glacier. It also dedicates its powerful capabilities to reinforcing the presidential belief that the original decision was correct. In a very real sense, the machinery has mechanisms that are potent in heading off any desire to change course. All of this traces back to the realization, subconscious or otherwise, that during his term of office, the president *is* the United States. Whatever argument he gets is unlikely to come from the internal structure of government, and when it *does* come that way, it is easy for him to close his ears to it. He may get an occasional argument on how best to carry out a policy; but rarely, if ever, that the policy he has set should be abandoned.

Were this a simple question of sycophancy, it could be handled administratively. Unfortunately, the problem is far deeper than the machinations of courtiers. They do exist in large numbers but most of their energies are absorbed in grabbing for personal favors and building havens of retreat for the future. Generally speaking, they play the role in the White House of the court jesters of the Middle Ages and may even be useful in that they give the chief executive badly needed relaxation. Paradoxically, it is the advisers who are *not* sycophantic, who are *not* looking for snug harbors, and who *do* feel the heavy weight of responsibility who are the most likely to play the reinforcing role. It is precisely because they recognize the ultimacy of the office that they react the way they do. However they feel, the burden of decision is on another man. Therefore, however much they may argue against a policy at its beginning stages, once it is set they become "good soldiers" and devote their time to making it work. Those who disagree strongly tend to remain in the structure in the vain hope they can change it coupled with the certainty that they would become totally ineffectual if they left.

This is the bitter lesson we should have learned from Vietnam. In the early days of that conflict, it might have been possible to pull out. My most vivid memories are the meetings early in Lyndon Johnson's presidency in which his advisers (virtually all holdovers from the Kennedy administration) were looking to him for guidance on how to proceed. He, on the other hand, felt an obligation to continue the Kennedy policies and he was looking to them for indications of what steps would carry out such a course. I will always believe that someone misread a signal from the other side with the resultant commitment to full-scale fighting. After that, all the resources of the federal government were devoted to advising the president on how to do what it was thought he wanted to do.

There were of course dissenting voices, a few of which reached the presidential presence, if not the presidential ear. (Presidents all develop an amazing capability to sleep with their eyes wide open when someone is saying something they do not want to hear.) In an earlier age, a man such as Undersecretary of State George Ball, who made his opposition to Vietnam known directly to the president, might have had some influence. But now all he could do was argue against the enormous reams of statistics that came from the Defense Department and other agencies. His words were literally swept away by the massive character of bureaucratic analysis pouring in on Johnson. It was not until a very subtle operator who understood the machinery—Clark Clifford—got his hands upon the Pentagon that the White House viewpoint was changed.

At no time during this process was there anything resembling a "plot" or a palace guard razzle-dazzle. The president was not conned into taking any of the steps that he took nor can anyone fairly be said to have hoodwinked him. All the bureaucrats were doing was concentrating their intellectual energies on searching for ways to carry out his decisions. This left little, or no, room for chewing over what had already been decided. Actually, the nature of modern technical, social, and political analysis is such that when the answers emerge they put an end to speculative thought rather than encouraging a further inquiry. Nothing illustrates this point more powerfully than the Vietnam war.

While I was in the White House, I developed an early skepticism toward the so-called kill ratios, the comparative statistics on the number of combatants slain on each side. My army experience had taught me that no company grade officer is going to risk his men by sending them into the boondocks to count bodies for some 4F clerk in a rear echelon. But I did believe in the pacification figures—the statistics that supposedly demonstrated an increasing control of the South Vietnamese government over villages once dominated by the Viet Cong. They seemed realistic to me. They were based on such questions as could the village headman sleep in his village at night; had the villagers recently paid taxes to the Viet Cong; did the villagers dare to leave their compounds at night; etc. I knew the federal government well enough to be certain that the people gathering those statistics were not lying. Consequently, they must have validity.

The rude awakening came shortly after I left the White House. I ran into a friend whom I had not seen in many years. We repaired to the nearest bar to catch up on old times and it turned out that he had been one of the people gathering the basic statistics for the pacification reports. When he told me that there were so many villages on his beat that he could spend no more than two hours a month in any one of them, I began to wonder. And when I learned that he spoke no Vietnamese and his French was indifferent, a light dawned. A picture formed in my mind of this "long nose" (a Southeast Asian term for Westerner) standing in the middle of a village where everyone wanted to get rid of him. As long as he was there, he was a menace. The Viet Cong might lob in a shell; a wrong answer might bring a raid from government troops; anyone who smiled at him might be visited that night for some remedial education. What was the quickest way of getting rid of him? Tell him what he wanted to hear. What does he want to hear? Whatever makes Saigon happy. What makes Saigon happy? Whatever makes the Pentagon happy. What makes the Pentagon happy? Whatever makes the situation room of the White House happy. What makes the people in the situation room of the White House happy? Whatever makes the president happy—as though you needed to ask.

In short, those figures in which I believed were almost certainly nothing but sonar echoes of the president's hopes and dreams. They were disguised, of course, because they were consolidated in Saigon and reevaluated in the Pentagon. That means that by the time they landed on the president's desk they had the authority and persuasive qualities of the Sermon on the Mount and the laws of the Medes and the Persians. In the whole process, nobody was lying, except the people in the village. There was just uncritical acceptance of figures. By that time, I had had enough experience among Indians in South America to learn the uncanny ability of a subordinate people to read the minds of the masters, and this was a perfect example.

My friend's information started a train of conjecture. How valid were *any* of the figures out of Vietnam? I never had—and do not now have—suspicions that they were fictitious. But they were all based on "assumptions" —and assumptions control the answers that one gets from a computer. Personally, I believe that the Delphic Oracle was a much more useful device for solving a society's problems. It gave mystical answers to questions, which made people think hard to solve the mysteries. Often they lit upon the right answers to the problems as well as to the mysteries. The computer gives one final answer and, if it is wrong, God help all of us.

In talking to friends about the presidency, I have found the hardest point to explain is that setbacks often impel presidents to redouble their efforts without changing their policies. This seems to be perversity because very few of us have the opportunity to make decisions of colossal consequences. When our projects go wrong, it is not too difficult for most of us to shrug our shoulders, cut our losses, and take off on a new tack. Our egos may be bruised. But we can live with that. It is a different thing altogether when we can give orders that can lead to large-scale death and destruction or even to economic devastation. Such a situation brings into play psychological factors that are virtually unconquerable.

Suppose, for example, that a president gives the military an order that leads to the deaths of several soldiers in combat. Can any human being who did such a thing say to himself: "Those men are dead because I was a God-damned fool! Their blood is on my hands." The more likely thought is: "Those men died in a noble cause and we must see to it that their sacrifice was not in vain." This, of course, could well be the "right" answer. But even if it is the wrong answer, it is virtually certain to be the one that will be accepted. Therefore, more men are sent and then more and then more. Every death makes a pull out more unacceptable.

Furthermore, when a large amount of blood has been spilled, a point can be reached where popular opposition to a policy will actually spur a president to redoubled effort in its behalf. This is due to the aura of history that envelops every occupant of the Oval Office. He lives in a museum, a structure dedicated to preserving the greatness of the American past. He walks the same halls paced by Lincoln waiting feverishly for news from Gettysburg or Richmond. He dines with silver used by Woodrow Wilson as he pondered the proper response to the German declaration of unrestricted submarine warfare. He has staring at him constantly portraits of the heroic men who faced the same excruciating problems in the past that he is facing in the present. It is only a matter of time until he feels himself a member of an exclusive community whose inhabitants never finally leave the mansion. When stories leaked out that Richard Nixon was "talking to the pictures" in the White House, it was taken by many as evidence that he was cracking up. To anyone who has had the opportunity to observe a president at close range, it is perfectly normal conduct.

Obviously, this is a situation that tends to persuade presidents that the successes of their predecessors afford guides to coping with today's problems. If Abraham Lincoln held on despite counsel to the contrary during the darkest days of the Civil War, then his twentieth-century successor should hang on during the darkest days of Vietnam. What is less obvious is that a president will almost certainly reach a state in which the White House community will extend forward, as well as backward, in time. If the past is real and present, so is the future real and present. Will his successors feel *his* presence? Will his successors look to *him* for guidance in their problems? Does he not have an obligation to set for them an example of courage and vision when all around him lesser men are calling for retreat? In effect, the criteria for how he conducts himself in office will be set by "history" rather than by contemporaries. When this happens, the voices of dissent—no matter how many decibles they are raising—fade from the grounds of the executive mansion.

In recent years, the obsession of presidents with unwritten history reached epic proportions. It can best be seen in the presidential libraries, which Lewis Mumford appropriately compares to the Egyptian pyramids. They began on a very modest basis when Herbert Hoover, without fanfare, donated his papers to the Stanford University Library. This was followed by a somewhat more ambitious project in which Franklin Roosevelt established a presidential library at Hyde Park. Harry Truman was next with a building that contained not only his papers but a replica of the Oval Office. Dwight Eisenhower selected Gettysburg for his monument and John Kennedy Harvard University. Lyndon Johnson topped everyone with a building that contained a museum and more papers than any other. This was the high point of the crescendo. Richard Nixon had difficulty finding someone to accept his papers, and his successors have been somewhat more modest in their contributions.

The libraries are, of course, useful to scholars. I am not citing them in any critical sense. But the fact remains that the impulse that has led to their construction has more of an affinity to Ramses II or Louis XIV than to Duns Scotus or Immanuel Kant. They reflect a man who feels that he is joining a Pantheon of Immortals and wishes to leave behind him visible symbols of his reign. They proclaim that the president is a king and the White House is a court.

For most of the American saga, the forces that foster a monarchical feeling did not have too much to work on. The problems were largely internal and presidents had little to do with the daily lives of citizens. Americans paid scant attention to the rest of the world and regarded Europe chiefly as a place from which they were happy they had escaped. The twentieth century made the difference. It gave our presidents a taste of what it meant to be an international figure and they eagerly took to their new role. Theodore Roosevelt dabbled in international negotiations and shaped the Treaty of Portsmouth, which ended the Russo-Japanese War. Woodrow Wilson led us into World War I and became the spark plug for the establishment of the League of Nations. In the latter instance, he went too far and was unable to secure acceptance of the League by the United States. Under Franklin Roosevelt, America became a superpower on the world scene. Presidents found themselves caught up in historic maneuvers on every continent and, in the process, the inherently monarchical qualities of their position came to the fore. It is worth taking a close look at that era.

Chapter III

The Foundations of Monarchy

TO UNDERSTAND THE institution of the presidency, one must first grasp the realization that the president and the nation are so intertwined that they cannot be distinguished from each other. During the four to eight years he is in office, the man in the Oval Room *is* the United States. When we say that America is intervening in Nicaragua, we mean that the *president* has ordered intervention in Nicaragua. When we say that America is exploring new avenues of conciliation in the Middle East, we mean that the *president* is exploring new avenues of conciliation in the Middle East. And when we say that U.S. representatives state the American position at an international conference, we mean that people appointed by the *president* are stating what *he* has decided should be stated at an international conference.

This is a heady atmosphere in which to live. It is one thing to operate an organization, another thing to be the symbolic cement that holds the organization together. Both jobs are within the realm of human capability, although, of course, both can become difficult as the organization increases in size. When the two are put together, however, they get in each other's way. The hard, sharp decisions needed to manage tend to become softened in deference to the symbolic role. And the soft, conciliatory words needed for unity are forced to yield to the harder language of management. What is even more important is that the God-like status of the dual role can easily separate a human being from social reality.

There are few warnings to the president-elect that this problem will be encountered. No one has placed over the White House door the admonition *"facile decensus Averni."* No one comes rushing to him with somber warnings and Dutch-uncle talk. The state of euphoria induced by political success is upon him at the very moment that caution, introspection, and humility are most needed. The process of erosion by which reality gradually fades begins when someone says, "Congratulations, Mr. President."

There is built into the presidency a series of devices that tend to remove the occupant of the Oval Office from all of the forces that require most men to rub up against the hard facts of life on a daily basis. The life of the White House is the life of a court. It is a structure designed for one purpose and one purpose only—to serve the material needs and the desires of a single man. It is felt that this man is grappling with problems of such tremendous consequence that every effort must be made to relieve him of the irritations that vex the average citizen. His mind, it is held, must be absolutely free of petty annoyances so that he can concentrate his faculties on the "great issues" of the day.

To achieve this end, every conceivable facility is made available, from the latest luxurious jet aircraft to a masseur constantly in attendance to soothe raw presidential nerves. Even more important, he is treated with all of the reverence due a monarch. No one—except possibly a court jester—interrupts presidential contemplation for anything less than a catastrophe. No one speaks to him unless spoken to first. No one ever invites him to "go soak your head" when his demands become petulant or unreasonable.

In theory, privilege is accorded to, and accepted by, a

man in accordance with his responsibilities. It is supposed to compensate for heavier burdens than those carried by lesser mortals. In practice, privilege justifies itself—every new perquisite automatically becomes a normal condition of life. Any president on entering office is startled—and a little abashed—at the privileges available to him. But in a matter of months they become part of an environment that he necessarily regards as his just and due entitlement—not because of the office but because of his mere existence. It is doubtful that even Harry S Truman—the most democratic of contemporary presidents—wore the same size hat when he left the White House as he did the day he entered.

This status was built into the American government by the Constitution itself. The Founding Fathers had rejected the concept of the divine right of monarchy. But when they sat down to write a constitution that would assure freedom, they were incapable of thinking of government in any terms other than monarchy. Someone, they reasoned, must reign and rule. Someone must give orders that cannot be questioned. Someone must have final authority. Therefore, their conclusion, although not stated in these terms, was a solution that placed in office a monarch but limited the scope of the monarch's activities.

In the context of the late eighteenth century, the solution was an excellent one. First, the Founding Fathers analyzed the functions of government and divided them into three basic categories—the determination of policy, the execution of policy, and the adjudication of disputes arising out of the determination and the execution. The determination of policy was granted to Congress and the adjudication of disputes to the judiciary. The execution of policy they lodged in the hands of the president and within that area they gave him, for all practical purposes, total authority, not so much by affirmation but by failing to set many boundaries on what he could do. They felt that by dividing functions they had created competing power centers within the government and that the competition would prevent any one center from assuming a monopoly of power. As an additional safeguard, they limited the term of the president to four years (with an option for renewal if mutually agreeable between the president and the electorate) and gave Congress the authority to remove the president from office, although only on the basis of cumbersome machinery.

The accent was on stability, and the firebrands of the Revolution—Tom Paine, Patrick Henry, James Otis—were given short shrift, the traditional fate of revolutionaries when men meet to put the pieces together after the crockery has been smashed. But the Founding Fathers were neither reactionary nor timorous. They provided—whether consciously, intuitively, or by sheer luck—ample room for the constitutional institutions to react in new ways to new circumstances, as long as the institutions themselves did not change in any fundamental respect. Generally, this objective was achieved by indirection.

The president, for example, was forbidden to legislate or adjudicate, but there was remarkably little definition of his executive powers. As a result, the strength of the president in office at any given time determined the extent of what he regarded as his mandate. It was inevitable that strong men such as Jackson, Lincoln, and the two Roosevelts would interpret the absence of specific prohibitions as the presence of specific authority and act accordingly. Harry Truman even invoked the doctrine of "inherent" presidential powers to seize the nation's steel mills despite the lack of any legislative authorization—an effort that did not succeed because his popular following at the time was far short of his own supply of willpower.

Of equal importance was the Founding Fathers' failure to provide a method of determining whether an act of Congress transgressed the permissible boundaries of the

Constitution. It was inevitable that such questions would arise and would be regarded differently by men whose function was to represent the popular will and men whose function was to administer a theoretically impersonal body of law. Had the doctrine of judicial review of legislative acts not been established by Chief Justice John Marshall, it is virtually certain that one of his successors would have done so. This particular gap was so huge that it had to be plugged somehow. But it is only a matter of time until a body that has succeeded in acquiring the power to forbid (which is essentially the power of the Supreme Court over Congress and the executive) also takes over the power to direct. This is the process that has made the judiciary a major agency for social change in the past three decades.

The framers of the Constitution had no way of foreseeing the effects of their most important decision—to give the presidency the functions of both chief of state and chief of government. It is doubtful that they were even aware that the functions could exist separately. They knew that there had to be someone to speak for all the government. They also knew that there had to be someone to manage the affairs of the country. The concept that these functions could be separated was alien to their experience, even though the origins of separation were already apparent in the relationship between the king of England and the prime minister.

They lived in a universe dominated by the concept of ownership and in which management independent of ownership was unknown. The parallel to government seemed obvious in their minds. Furthermore, they were confronted with an immediate and apparent problem that far overshadowed what could then be only abstract ideas of the distinction between reigning and ruling. They had a nation that was being pulled apart by the centrifugal forces of state pride. Their task was to devise some method by which thirteen quite independent political units could be merged into a collective whole. Their problem was to find some counterweight that would balance forces of disunity and induce Americans to think of themselves as citizens of the United States rather than as citizens of Connecticut, New York, Virginia, or Georgia. And they had to do it relatively quickly.

The most practical method of unifying people is to give them a symbol with which they all can identify. If the symbol is human, its efficacy is enhanced enormously. The obvious symbol was the president—the man who held the role of commander-in-chief of the armed forces, the man to whom all could pay respects as the first citizen. In short, the Founding Fathers established the presidency as a position of reverence and, as they were truly wise and sophisticated men, their efforts were as effective as human wisdom could make them.

The consequences of this decision were ultimately inescapable although not immediately discernible. In the simple society of eighteenth-century United States, it was not easy to conceive of the federal government in terms of grandeur. An Abigail Adams could hang her washing in the East Room; a Dolly Madison could act as a porter, running to safety with important works of art in advance of British occupation; an Andrew Jackson could invite all his frontier friends into the White House for a rollicking party where they trampled the official furniture with muddy boots and passed out on the plush carpets of the Oval Room. But even in a nation as close to the realities of the frontier as the United States, a position established to inspire awe and reverence would inevitably pick up the trappings of reverence. And the trappings could not fail to have an effect on the man whom they served as a buffer against the rest of the world.

Among the fundamental characteristics of monarchy is untouchability. Contact with the king is forbidden except to an extremely few people or as a rare privilege to be exercised on great occasions. The king's body is sanctified and not subject to violation by lesser mortals unless he himself so wishes. He is not to be jostled in crowds; he is not to be clapped on the back; he is not to be placed in danger of life or limb or even put to the annoyance of petty physical discomfort. Nor can he be compelled to account for his actions upon demand.

By the twentieth century, the presidency had taken on all the regalia of monarchy except robes, a scepter, and a crown. The president was not to be jostled by a crowd, unless he elected to subject himself to do so during those moments when he shed his role as chief of state and mounted the hustings as a candidate for reelection. The ritual of shaking hands with the president took on more and more the coloration of the medieval "king's touch" as a specific for scrofula. The president was not to be called to account by any other body (after the doctrine of executive privilege was established). In time, the ultimate hallmark of imperial majesty began to appear: Presidents referred to themselves more and more as "we."

These are the conditions under which a president-elect today enters office. In fact, the aura of majesty begins to envelop him the moment the electorate has decided on him. Trusted assistants who have been calling him by his first name for years switch immediately to the deferential "Mr. President." The Secret Service agents who protected him during the campaign are suddenly joined by their chiefs who, up to that point, have stayed away from him and the other candidates in order to emphasize their neutrality. Members of the Army Signal Corps almost silently appear with communications equipment such as he has never seen before. All these developments take place as he bathes in the universal congratulations that always come to the successful candidate, even from his bitterest opponents. The agents that corrupt the democratic soul creep into his life in the guise of enthusiastic supporters, tactful police officers, self-effacing telephone linemen, and well-trained house servants. Even the members of the press, for a few months at least, regard him with some awe. The apotheosis has begun.

During the early days of a president's incumbency, the atmosphere of reverence that surrounds him acquires validity in his own eyes because of the ease with which he can get results. Congress is eager to approve his nominees and pass his bills. Business is anxious to provide him with "friends" and assistants. Labor is ready to oblige him with a climate of industrial peace. Foreign ambassadors scurry to locate suitable approaches.

It is a wonderful and heady feeling to be a president—at least for the first few months.

The environment of deference, approaching sycophancy, helps to foster an insidious belief: that the president and a few of his most trusted advisers are possessed of a special knowledge that must be closely held within a small group lest the plans and the designs of the United States be anticipated and frustrated by enemies. It is a knowledge that is thought to be endangered in geometrical proportion to the number of other people to whom it is passed. Therefore, vital national projects can be worked out only within a select coterie, to prevent "leaks."

Obviously, there *is* information that a nation must keep to itself if it is to survive in the present world climate. Thus the number of minds that can be brought to bear on any given problem is often in inverse proportion to the importance of the problem.

The steps that led to the bombing of North Vietnam were discussed by a small group of men. They were men of keen perception and finely honed judgment. It is doubtful that any higher degree of intelligence could have been brought to bear on the problem. But no matter how fine the intelligence or how thoroughgoing the information available, the fact remained that none of these men was put to the test of defending his position in public debate. And it is amazing what even the best of minds discovers when forced to answer critical questions. Unfortunately, in this as in many other instances, the public comment came after, not before, irreversible commitment.

Of course, within these councils there was at least one "devil's advocate." But an official dissenter always starts with half his battle lost. It is assumed that he is bringing up arguments solely because arguing is his official role. It is understood that he is not going to press his points harshly or stridently. Therefore, his objections and cautions are discounted before they are delivered. But they are also welcomed because they prove for the record that decision was preceded by controversy and a consideration of all sides of the question.

As a general rule, the quality of judgment usually varies directly with the number of minds that are brought to bear upon an issue. No man is so wise as to play his own "devil's advocate," and workable wisdom is the distillation of many different viewpoints that have clashed heatedly and directly in an exchange of opinion. To maintain the necessary balance between assurances of security and assurances that enough factors have been taken into consideration is perhaps the most pressing problem of statecraft. The atmosphere of the White House, in which the president is treated constantly as an infallible and reverential object, is not the best in which to resolve this problem.

In retrospect, it is almost impossible to believe that John Kennedy embarked on the ill-fated Bay of Pigs venture. It was poorly conceived, poorly planned, poorly executed, and undertaken with grossly inadequate knowledge. But anyone who has ever sat in on a White House council can easily deduce what happened without knowing any facts other than those which appeared in the public press. White House councils are not debating matches in which ideas emerge from the heated exchanges of participants. The council centers around the president, himself, to whom everyone addresses his observations.

The first strong observations to attract the favor of the president become subconsciously the thoughts of everyone in the room. The focus of attention shifts from a testing of all concepts to a groping for means of overcoming the difficulties. A thesis that could not survive an undergraduate seminar in a liberal arts college becomes accepted doctrine, and the only question is not *whether* it should be done but *how* it should be done. A forceful public airing of the Bay of Pigs plan would have endangered the whole project, of course. It might also have prevented disaster.

On a different level can be cited the far less serious setback suffered by Lyndon Johnson when he attempted to merge the Commerce and the Labor departments into one agency. Out of a desire for a "surprise" headline, this proposal was held in the utmost secrecy between the president and his speech writers until a few moments before his State of the Union message was scheduled for delivery. Calls were made to the secretaries of labor and commerce. Pressed for a quick response they reacted as any government official reacts to such a call from the White House. They said, "Yes."

In a matter of days, it was apparent that the project had as much chance of getting off the ground as a kiwi. To organized labor, still headed by men with long memories, the Labor Department was a sacrosanct institution for which they had fought and bled in their youth. They had no intention of acquiescing to the removal from the cabinet of what they regarded as "our spokesman." Business, although less emotional, made it clear that industrialists did not relish the prospect of "our agency" being merged with what they regarded as the opposition. The president quietly buried the whole idea.

The truly baffling question, however, is how a man with the political sensitivity of Johnson could ever embark on such a futile enterprise. His success as the Senate Democratic leader had been based on his insistence on touching every base before launching a project. He was famous throughout the political community for "taking the temperature" of every affected group in advance and laying careful plans to meet any objections they might have before the objections were even raised. And yet here was an instance where even a perfunctory conversation with a few of his friends would have made clear that humiliation was the only conceivable outcome of his proposal.

The only conclusion that an observer can draw is that the atmosphere of the White House—the combination of sycophancy and a belief in the efficacy of closely held knowledge—had done its work. The man regarded as the outstanding politician of the mid-twentieth century had stepped into a buzzsaw that could have been foreseen by a wardheeler in any major city.

A reader of history will find innumerable and startling examples of political bloopers committed by men with records of political sagacity. How is one to explain Truman's inept handling of the Communist spy scare of the late 1940's, a mistake that opened up the era of Joe McCarthy? How is one to explain Franklin Roosevelt's futile effort to "pack" the Supreme Court? How is one to explain Woodrow Wilson's clumsy treatment of the Senate, which led directly to its refusal to permit United States participation in the League of Nations? None of these men had shown themselves politically inept on such a grand scale at any previous moment of their lives. It is an inference, but an inescapable one, that the White House is an institution that dulls the sensitivity of political men and ultimately reduces them to bungling amateurs in their basic craft—the art of politics.

The real question every president must ask himself is how he can resist the temptations of a process compounded of idolatry and lofty patriotic respect for a national symbol. By all the standards of past performance, he should be well equipped to face it. As a general rule, he has fought his way up through the political ranks. He has flattered and been flattered—and the mere fact that he has survived to the threshold of the White House should indicate a psychological capacity to keep flattery in perspective. He has dealt with rich people, poor people, wise people, fools, patriots, knaves, scoundrels, and wardheelers. Had he not maintained his perspective on human beings generally, it is doubtful that he would have received his party's nomination.

But the atmosphere of the White House is a heady one. It is designed to bring to its occupant privileges that are commensurate with the responsibilities he must bear. A privilege is, by definition, a boon not accorded to other people. And to the extent that a man exercises his privileges, he removes himself from the company of lesser breeds who must stand in line and wait their turn on a share-and-share-alike basis for the comforts of life. To a president, all other humans are "lesser breeds."

Furthermore, a president would have to be a dull clod indeed to regard himself without a feeling of awe. The atmosphere of the White House is calculated to instill in any man a sense of destiny. He literally walks in the footsteps of hallowed figures—of Jefferson, of Jackson, of Lincoln. The almost sanctified relics of a distant, semimythical past surround him as ordinary household objects to be used by his family. From the moment he enters the halls he is made aware that he has become enshrined in a pantheon of semidivine mortals who have shaken the world, and that he has taken from their hands the heritage of American dreams and aspirations.

Unfortunately for him, divinity, although it serves as a unifying quality, is a better basis for inspiration than it is for government. The world can be shaken from Mount Olympus but the gods were notoriously inefficient when it came to directing the affairs of mankind. The Greeks were wise about such matters. In their remarkable body of lore, human tragedy usually originated with divine intervention and their invocations to the deities were usually prayers of propitiation—by all that is holy, leave us alone!

A semidivinity is also a personification of a people, and presidents cannot escape the process. The trouble with personification is that it depends on abstraction and, in the course of the exercise, individual living people somehow get lost. The president becomes the nation, and when he is insulted, the nation is insulted; when he has a dream, the nation has a dream; when he has an antagonist, the nation has an antagonist.

It may well be that at some point it will no longer be necessary for nations to personify themselves in terms of a single human being. Many lesser forms of organization have already reached that stage of their social development—notably business. But even though I believe I can see incipient political trends moving in that direction, we are not there yet. We still require a symbol of unity and legitimacy. We are not going to be held together by rational discussion—as anyone knows who has ever attended a meeting of academics. For any assemblage of people to act as a unit, there must be some quasi-divine being who can be invoked at critical junctures. In our country that is the president—a man who can be challenged for what he *does* but not for what he *is*. His status is unassailable whatever the constituents may think about his abilities.

This is the essence of monarchy—to be a nation and to manage its affairs at the same time. At one point in history, monarchs were unchallengeable both in terms of status and operating control. During the Age of Enlightenment, this came to be considered a highly dubious proposition. It was discovered very quickly, however, that the symbol of unity was still needed. Some nations—notably Great Britain and its imitators—solved the problem by separating the two functions. They lodged the question of symbolic values with a constitutional monarch (or powerless president) and of operational control with a prime minister. Other nations—notably the Soviet Union with Josef Stalin—retained the dual role for one man but changed the base on which he was selected. In the United States, we performed an interesting experiment—we founded a nation in which we retained the dual role of the leader but severely circumscribed his powers and required him to undergo review every four years. The question is whether a plan that has worked so well up to now must be changed.

Chapter IV

What Does a President Do?

BEFORE GOING FURTHER, it is well to pause and ponder what seems to be a simple question: What does a president do? Almost everyone is positive that he or she knows the answer. But, in my experience, when people are asked to give specifics, they wind up stammering. The simplicity of the question is deceptive. The president is many different things at many different times. His position as the focal point of our society is easy to define. But what he does as that focal point is largely up to him. The Constitution is remarkably vague about his duties and leaves him with a lot of elbow room.

There are plenty of checks on his conduct. Congress can deny him legal authority to proceed in many directions, and where legalities are irrelevant, halt him in his tracks by denying money. The courts can declare his actions illegal and mandate that he follow different courses. In practice, however, Congress can act only when it can assemble a majority—a slow and often painful process— and the courts can enter the scene only when cases are brought before them. The president has the power of the initiative, and a bold man with an acute sense of timing can always find ways of exercising that power so that the rest of the government must go along. Once programs are set in motion, they acquire a momentum that makes it difficult to stop them.

The presidents who have captured the public imagination have been the bold ones. It is not difficult to call the roll. As the first chief executive, George Washington's name would have been historic anyway. But it did not hurt him to make it clear that he regarded himself and his papers as immune from Congressional prying. Thomas Jefferson had tremendous intellect but his greatest contribution to his country was his legally questionable purchase of the Louisiana Territory. Andrew Jackson constantly presented the Supreme Court with dilemmas and refused to enforce decisions he did not like. Abraham Lincoln suspended many of the basic liberties provided by the Constitution when he thought it necessary to do so in order to carry on the Civil War. Teddy Roosevelt sent the Navy—the Great White Fleet—halfway around the world on a saber-rattling expedition after Congress had refused funds for the trip. He then asked the House of Representatives and the Senate to appropriate money for the rest of the itinerary or else leave the fleet far from our shores. Woodrow Wilson embroiled the United States in Mexico and Central America with acts clearly outside the rules of conduct among nations (such as seizing the customs house at Veracruz). Franklin Roosevelt intervened openly on the side of Great Britain in World War II when the U.S. was presumably neutral, and then he persuaded Congress to authorize him to do what he had already done without authority.

The sweep of these actions was breathtaking. The great presidents did things that were extraordinary, and as a result a mythology surrounds the White House. One of the myths is that the office somehow ennobles the occupant. This concept probably achieved its most articulate expression in a book and a movie, *Gabriel Over the White House* (now mercifully forgotten), which was the favorite reading and viewing of millions during the early days of the New Deal.

Those who hold this idea are fond of referring to Harry Truman and his unexpected rise (as they see it) from a small-town machine politician to a world statesman possessed of rare qualities of courage and high purpose. They are less fond of references to Warren Harding and Calvin Coolidge, who left the presidency looking very little, if any, different from when they entered office.

In reality, the office neither elevates nor degrades a man. What it does is to provide a stage upon which all of his personality traits are magnified and accentuated. The aspects of his character that were not noted previously are not new. They were merely hidden from view in lesser positions, where he was only one of many politicians competing for public attention. It is absurd to contend that Truman's great courage and patriotism—the most noteworthy of his attributes—came to him when he walked into the Oval Office. The truth, which would be borne out by all of his intimates, is that he always possessed such qualities. But who would notice them in a senator from Missouri, particularly a senator who cared little about the techniques of public relations?

A president is one of the few figures in political life who is not regarded in terms of stereotypes. A senator who comes to Washington is quickly put into the class of liberal, conservative, or moderate (the latter usually meaning nondescript). These labels are not truly descriptive of his political ideology but of the symbols that he uses. The stereotypes are useful because without them it would be difficult for the press to analyze events. But they have a tendency to obscure the person. Lyndon Johnson's espousal of civil rights and welfare legislation as president came as a surprise to many people because they had spent a number of years looking at a label instead of a person. And Dwight Eisenhower's warning against the military-industrial complex seemed out of character because of the popular mythology that had portrayed him as a well-meaning but not particularly bright army general. Neither of the men changed when he entered the White House. Nobody had really looked at them before.

In actuality, a man's character and personality are not of the same concern in relation to his role as a senator or a member of the House of Representatives as they are to the role of the presidency. In Congress he is only one of a large group of advocates, and the end product of his activities will be tempered by his need for arriving at an accommodation with the others.

Presidential performance is an entirely different matter. In the White House, character and personality are important because no other limitations govern a man's conduct. Restraint must come from within the presidential soul and prudence from within the presidential mind. The adversary forces that temper the actions of others do not come into play until it is too late to change course.

Richard E. Neustadt has observed that expertise in presidential power "seems to be the province not of politicians as a class but of extraordinary politicians." The point is well taken and I suggest only a minor modification. The last few words should read "extraordinary men who have become politicians." This suggestion is put forward to emphasize the importance of personality to the success of a president. His character is the key to his success or failure in terms of history more than his ability to do the job.

Despite the widespread belief to the contrary, there is far less to the presidency, in terms of essential activity, than meets the eye. The psychological burdens are heavy, even crushing, but no president ever died of overwork and it is doubtful that any ever will. The chief executive can, of course, fill his working hours with as much motion as he desires. The "crisis" days (the American hostages held in Iran or the attempted torpedoing of American navy vessels in the Gulf of Tonkin) keep office lights burning into the midnight hours. But in terms of actual administration, the presidency is pretty much what the president wants to make of it. He can delegate the "work" to subordinates and reserve for himself only the powers of decision as did Eisenhower, or he can insist on maintaining tight control over every minor detail, like Lyndon Johnson.

The concept of the president who works around the clock is embedded deep in American mythology, however, and, with the exception of Eisenhower, presidents have agreed that it must be maintained. Even in the case of Eisenhower, his assistants thought they had to keep up appearances regardless of their chief's disdain for dissimulation. Jim Haggerty, his press secretary, was notorious for "saving up" official papers and announcements to release while the president was on vacation— thus preserving the illusion that it was a combination work-and-play holiday.

This led to a now outdated tradition in the press office of preparing "a day in the life of the president" for handling the queries of reporters burdened with this story by unsophisticated editors. It was usually labeled a "typical" day, with the date unspecified. Care was taken not to put two major and well-publicized events together in the list allowing someone to spot a discrepancy (i.e., don't combine a major announcement of more troops for Vietnam with an important—and announced—meeting of the National Security Council that happened two weeks later). A press secretary scratching for a believable schedule quickly found out how few "working" events actually took place and usually fell back on a day when the president had received, and accepted the credentials of, ten ambassadors (three minutes each) and inserted into the list "worked at his desk for three hours."

Another measurement of the "workload" can be found in the long-standing custom of the White House press office of scouring the executive agencies for items to release to the newspaper correspondents. This practice has led generations of information officers to the verge of rebellion because of the obvious fact that if an item is unknown *to* the White House in the normal course of events, it is probably an item that should not be released *from* the White House anyway. Nevertheless, the practice has continued and newspaper reporters have found themselves bombarded daily with releases on waterfowl conservation, minor grants for pollution abatement, and education projects for Indian reservations. Such releases rarely make headlines, but their sheer bulk creates the impression of unending activity on the part of the president.

The concept of the overburdened president represents one of the insidious forces that serve to separate the chief executive from the real universe of living, breathing, troubled human beings. It is the basis for encouraging his most outrageous expressions, for pampering his most childish tantrums, and for fostering his most arrogant actions. More than anything else, it serves to create an environment in which no man can live for any considerable length of time and retain his psychological balance.

A president can be rude, insulting, and even downright sadistic to his closest advisers and their only response will be: "How fortunate that he has people around him who understand the tremendous burdens he is carrying." He can display the social manners of a Vandal sacking a Roman villa and his intimates will remark to one another: "We don't care about style. The only thing that is important is his deep feeling for the urban poor. Of course, he is somewhat crude but what does that matter?" He can elevate a mediocre sycophant to a high position and members of his entourage will remark: "You know, it is amazing how perceptive and socially conscious that young man is!"

The burdens would be lighter, the urban poor would be better served, and the young men might be more perceptive and socially conscious if presidents had to face the same minor social penalties that the rest of us do. An occasional "go soak your head" or "that's stupid" would clear the murky, turgid atmosphere of the White House and let in some health-giving fresh air.

This, however, is not likely. A president moves through his days surrounded by literally hundreds of people whose relationship to him is that of a doting mother to a spoiled child. Whatever he wants is brought to him immediately—food, drink, helicopters, airplanes, people, in fact, everything but relief from his political problems. And the assistant who is unable to provide a requested service—no matter how unreasonable—automatically blames his own shortcomings rather than external circumstances.

The system feeds upon itself. Impossible demands that cannot be met breed guilt feelings that serve as a basis for rationalizing even more impossible demands. It is little wonder that after they leave office White House assistants need a period of decompression, in which they can reestablish their own egos, even more than does the president.

The presidential burden does not lie in the workload. It stems from the crushing responsibility of political decisions, with life and death literally hanging in the balance for millions of people. A president is haunted every waking hour of his life by the fear that he has taken the wrong turn, selected the wrong course, issued the wrong orders. In the realm of political decision he can turn to no one for authoritative counsel. Only *he* is authoritative. The situation was summed up by the sign Truman kept on his desk: "The Buck Stops Here."

Every reflective human being eventually realizes that his heaviest burdens are not the responsibilities he bears for himself but the responsibilities he bears for others. Where the load becomes too heavy, he can walk out if no one else is affected. The escape process becomes difficult when his family is involved. And as the number of people dependent on him increases, leaving becomes impossible. The president's responsibilities literally embrace—either positively or negatively—every living person. There is no escape, no place to hide—not even for a moment.

Those who seek to lighten the burdens of the presidency by easing the workload do the occupant of that office no favor. The "workload"—and especially the ceremonial workload—are the events of a president's day that make life endurable. These are his only opportunities to concentrate his mental processes on problems that are amenable to technical solution—and thereby blot out of his consciousness the image of napalm exploding through the houses of an Asian village at his order; of hungry people walking the streets because he might have misused his fiscal authority; of angry opponents sharpening political knives in anticipation of revenge for a slight that he inflicted in a moment of irritation; of jeering cartoons and sneering slogans held aloft on giant placards by college youth alienated because he increased the draft quotas. Work is a blessed relief that comes all too rarely.

It is difficult to pinpoint this phenomenon, as it does not yield readily to quantitative analysis. It is impossible to take a day and divide it with any sure sense of confidence into "working hours" and "nonworking hours." But it is apparent from the large volume of words that have been written about presidents that in the past few decades, the only one who seemed able to relax completely was Eisenhower. He was capable of taking a vacation for the sake of enjoying himself, and he disdained any suggestion that he was acting otherwise.

Franklin Roosevelt apparently had little or no time to devote to relaxation. He was notorious for using his dinner hours as a means of lobbying bills through Congress. Once Harry Truman had made a decision he was able to put it out of his mind and proceed to another problem. Furthermore, he too disdained any pretensions of working when he wasn't. But those who were close to him made it clear that he really didn't know what to do with himself when he took a holiday. His favorite resort was Key West, Florida, where he would "go fishing" —but he would hold a rod only if someone put it in his hands, and about all he really enjoyed was the sunshine and the opportunity to take long walks.

John Kennedy was described as a "compulsive reader" who could not pass up any written document regardless of its relevance to his problems or its contents. Many of his intimates reported that any spare time would find him restlessly prowling the White House looking for something to read. Lyndon Johnson anticipated with horror long weekends in which there was nothing to do. He usually spent Saturday afternoons in lengthy conferences with newspaper reporters who were hastily summoned from their homes to spend hours listening to Johnson expound the thesis that his days were so taken up with the nation's business that he had no time to devote to friends.

The real misery of the average presidential day is the haunting knowledge that decisions have been made on incomplete information and inadequate counsel. Tragically, the information must *always* be incomplete and the counsel *always* inadequate, for in the arena of human activity in which a president operates there are no quantitative answers. He must deal with those problems for which the computer offers no solution, those disputes where rights and wrongs are so inextricably mixed that the righting of every wrong creates a new wrong, those divisions which arise out of differences in human desires rather than differences in the available facts, those crisis moments in which action is imperative and cannot wait upon orderly consideration. He has no guideposts other than his own philosophy and intuition, and if he is devoid of either, no one can substitute. Other people can tell

him "what I would do if I were president." But those
other people are *not* president. Try as they may, they
cannot achieve that sense of personal identification with
history which is the hallmark of the chief executive.
Presidents are wont to explain those of their decisions
which are incomprehensible to their contemporaries on
the grounds that they have access to information not
available in its entirety to others. The inference is: "If
you knew what I knew, you would understand why I did
what I did." That a president has more comprehensive
data available to him is true (or at least can be true if a
president pays sufficient attention to his sources of information) but irrelevant. On sweeping policy decisions,
which are, after all, relatively few, a president makes up
his mind on the basis of the same *kind* of information
that is available to the average citizen. When Franklin
Roosevelt decided to commit the U.S. against the Axis
powers in World War II he had little relevant information on the Nazis, the Fascists, and the Japanese war-
lords that was qualitatively different from that which
could be gleaned from *The New York Times*. When Harry
Truman decided to resist Communist aggression in Korea, he knew very little more than that the forty-ninth
parallel had been crossed by Communist troops, a fact
that was already in headlines. When Lyndon Johnson
decided to send troops into the Dominican Republic, he
had no information advantage over his fellow Americans
other than a brief telephone conversation with his ambassador (although later, reams of factual data were gathered to justify the action).

Of course, a president usually *knows* more about the
situation than other people—not because he has more
information but because it is his *business* to know and
people usually pay attention to their business. He has the
responsibility of making ultimate decisions that will be
submitted to the harshest judgment possible—the judg-

ment of history. This is the kind of prospect that tends to concentrate a man's mind wonderfully.

Moreover, the difference in the decision-making process between the president and his fellow Americans is not necessarily that he has taken better advantage of the available facts than we have but that he, and only he, must make the decision. As it is his business to *know*, it is his exclusive business to *decide*. This gives his thought processes a quality that no other person, not even his most trusted adviser, can have. His fellow Americans stand in the position of critics. They can second guess, they can be Monday morning quarterbacks. Quite possibly they will have judgments demonstrably superior to those made by the president. But they do not have to say "yes" or "no" under pressure of a deadline. They do not have to take responsibility for action in the sure knowledge that the action will produce consequences that will demonstrate to the whole world that they were right or wrong. Neither do they have to offer leadership to diverse groups of people who are strong-willed and convinced of their own righteousness.

A president is many things. Basically, however, his functions fall into two categories. First, and perhaps most important, he is the symbol of the legitimacy and the continuity of our government. It is only through him that power can be exercised effectively—but only until opposition forces rally themselves to counter it. Second, he is the political leader of our nation. He must resolve the policy questions that will not yield to quantitative, empirical analysis and then persuade enough of his countrymen of the rightness of his decisions so that they are carried out without disrupting the fabric of society.

At the present time, neither of these functions can be carried out without the president. The analytical techniques of the social sciences have yet to replace the intuitive judgment of the politician on the time and place for taking certain steps. And even if such techniques could be devised, the president would still be needed to legitimize the decisions of the analysts. The voters place in the White House a man, not an electronic computer.

The difference between the great and the mediocre presidents probably centers on each one's ability to grasp this point. The great presidents understood the White House as a focal point of power from which flowed the decisions that shaped the destiny of the nation. They realized that their day-to-day activities are intended to bolster support for policies, to obtain the backing that could translate their judgment into meaningful action, and to deal with the conflicting forces that lie within our society in such a way that they could be reduced to common denominators and therefore to a degree of coherence. The mediocre presidents, on the other hand, have tended to regard the White House as a stage for the presentation of performances to the public or as a fitting honor to cap a career that was illlustrious in some other field.

It is doubtful that Franklin Roosevelt made a single speech as president that did not have a specific political objective. Sometimes his timing was wrong (as in the 1937 "quarantine the aggressors" speech in which he unsuccessfully tried to lead the nation out of isolationism). Sometimes his timing was superb (as in his "little dog Fala" speech, which blasted Thomas Dewey out of the presidential race in 1944). But always there was an objective, a reason other than a display of rhetoric for making a speech.

It is not my intention here to name the mediocre presidents. But the reader is invited to inspect the speeches made by those whom he or she considers in that category. It will become quickly apparent that most of these speeches were made solely for the occasion rather than for their impact.

A brief look should be taken at the nature of decision making in the White House. On few other governmental subjects have so many words been lavished. It is assumed that there is something called a "decision-making process" that can be charted in much the same fashion as the table of organization for a business corporation. The fondest dream of the political scientist is to trace this flow chart in such a way that it will be available for study, comment, criticism, and possibly improvement. It may be that such a process existed during the Eisenhower administration. Certainly, this was a widespread impression at the time. It was stated by writer after writer that Ike had introduced the military staff-and-command system to the presidency and that a filtering process examined all the options and eventually presented them to him in the form of a one-page paper upon which he could inscribe "yes" or "no." This has been repeated so many times with so little dispute that it is probably a fact, although anyone who has had White House service will forever after be skeptical of the pictures that are painted on the outside. But if so, it was a development that occurred only once in recent years.

The fact is that a president makes his decisions as he wishes to make them, under conditions that he himself has established, and at times of his own determination. He decides what he wants to decide. Any student of the White House who believes that he will make a contribution to political thought by analyzing the process is sadly mistaken. At best—at the very best—he can contribute to human knowledge only some insights into the decision-making process of one man.

Presidents glory in telling people that they are prisoners of a system and of circumstances beyond their control. This is probably the subconscious device by which the chief executive prepares his alibi for history. It is true that a president must deal with forces and circumstances that he did not create and that he cannot ignore. But how he deals with them is up to him. A president, in a peculiar sense that does not apply to other people, is the master of his own fate and the captain of his own soul. If Congress is balky, this is a political problem and a president is supposedly a political expert. If information is inadequate, the president has at his command a federal establishment of at least 2,500,000 people over which he has virtually undisputed authority. If foreign relations are contentious and unruly, this is merely one of the conditions under which he operates and not a "reason" for failure.

There was no categorical imperative that required William McKinley to declare war on Spain, Woodrow Wilson to serve an ultimatum on Germany, John Kennedy to order the invasion of the Bay of Pigs, or Lyndon Johnson to increase American forces in Vietnam from 20,000 to 500,000. These were all decisions made by human beings who had other options. Whether they were right or wrong is a matter that will not be discussed here. The relevant point is that none of these presidents was a prisoner of history at the moment of truth. They may have been prisoners of psychological forces from their childhood, of racial and ethnic memories, of environments that molded their thinking and conditioned their reflexes. But whatever psychic forces may have been playing on them, they could all have said "no."

This is a point well worth bearing in mind. The essence of the presidency is the responsibility for making decisions and the necessity for making them without peers—with advice and counsel, yes; but also in the sure knowledge that the president alone bears the full and complete burden.

Chapter V

The Power of the Initiative

THE AWESOME POWER potential lodged in the presidency did not manifest itself for more than a century. First, the federal establishment had not reached a size where its sheer numbers made it a political factor, and it did not have functions which reached into the daily lives of citizens. Second, it was not a century of crisis which could be solved only in Washington. When such crises did arise—as in the Civil War—the capacity of the chief executive to override all other considerations in our society became apparent at once. Once the crisis had been overcome, the president retired into obscurity (who can name the five presidents who followed Abraham Lincoln?).

The twentieth century has been an altogether different proposition. It has been characterized by the increasing participation of the United States in world affairs. This was a natural and inevitable step. But it had unforeseen consequences. As the participation increased, so did vulnerability to world crisis. And the one rule that is absolute is that the president's power becomes predominate in times of trouble. The executive is the only agency that can act, and the normal rules of society are regarded as niceties until the crisis is over. This made the mid-twentieth century an ideal stage for the emergence of the president in all his monarchical glory. In the fields of foreign affairs and national security, the president has more elbow room, and a daring man can do much with the power of the initiative.

The president's power is subject to certain checks. But in the field of foreign affairs and defense, these checks are almost entirely in the nature of a review. Theoretically, Congress can always hamper his activities by refusing to grant the necessary appropriations to pay for the acts taken by the executive. But it is inconceivable, for instance, that Congress would refuse appropriations to support soldiers who are fighting in the name of their country's freedom. It is also inconceivable that Congress would withhold appropriations essential to sustain the nation's prestige. And it is even more inconceivable that Congress would fail to approve a president's action against an avowed enemy.

The war in Vietnam rested for years on the Gulf of Tonkin Resolution, which gave carte blanche to Lyndon Johnson to take virtually unprecedented steps in Southeast Asia. Some senators have since stated that had they known what was to follow, they would not have voted for it. This is not only hindsight but nonsense. The resolution was passed following a presumed effort to torpedo an American naval vessel in the Gulf of Tonkin and after strong U.S. air retaliation against North Vietnamese torpedo boats in Haiphong. It is unthinkable that very many members of Congress would have been willing under such circumstances to tell the world that the United States would not support its leader in a moment of national peril (in fact, only two senators took that course).

In domestic affairs, the president's power of initiative is far less effective. This is simply because few domestic crises require an immediate affirmation of national unity. In the domestic field, Congress is willing to repudiate a president because this is something that rests within the family. It does not assume that catastrophe will follow clear evidence of division. Even here, presidents have developed techniques that give them an initiative over the legislative branch of the government. These include preparation of the budget, at which Congress can only nitpick; the establishment of revolving funds, which go a long way toward negating the appropriation authority; and the use of executive orders, which have limited force of law but which can completely bypass Congress.

A most dramatic example of the latter was the executive order by which John Kennedy set up an Equal Employment Opportunity Commission that had far more drastic authority to enforce nondiscrimination than could have been accorded to a legally established Fair Employment Practices Commission. This was done by the simple device of permitting the commission to initiate contract cancellation for contractors held to be guilty of racial discrimination in hiring practices. Congress has no adequate countermeasures to such an act. It can only react, and although the reaction can be violent, that is not equivalent to having the edge that comes with the initiative.

Almost, but not quite, as important as the power of the initiative is the chief executive's ability to place his views before the public. This is one arena in which he has no equal from the standpoint of opportunity. When he has a point of view, that point of view can be communicated instantly to the American people, and it has behind it all the power of the nation speaking through the voice of one individual. Furthermore, the president has the capability of shaping his words as he wants them without the necessity of sifting them through a "committee" process, which hampers any similar expression of views on the part of the Congress or the courts.

The president's ability to place his views before the public is important primarily because he can usually set the terms of the national debate—and anyone who can set the terms of a debate can win it. An outstanding example is the manner in which Harry Truman converted certain defeat into unexpected victory in 1948.

At the beginning of the year, no one conceded Truman any chance for reelection. He had been plagued by deep divisions within the Democratic party and by the strains placed on the economy by the postwar readjustment. In 1946 the voters had signaled their disapproval by the election of the first Republican Congress in fourteen years, and there was no reason to believe that they were dissatisfied with their decision. The situation was so serious that leading Democrats debated the almost unheard-of possibility of denying renomination to Truman—a step rarely taken in our history. Important party leaders had even proposed that General Eisenhower be asked to be the Democratic standard bearer (at that time no one had any idea of Eisenhower's politics). The Democratic convention in Philadelphia was disspirited and lackluster, with the only heartening note a remarkable speech by Senator Alben W. Barkley of Kentucky—a speech that secured for him the vice-presidential nomination. There was, of course, no real alternative to Truman's renomination, and the delegates went along reluctantly.

But Truman was a fighter. He startled the convention and the country by declaring immediate war on the "do-nothing, good-for-nothing, Republican-controlled, Eightieth Congress." He whistle-stopped the nation, lambasting the Republican Congress at every crossroads and every train station. The issue became the Congress itself, and Thomas Dewey, the Republican candidate, who considered his victory a foregone conclusion, made the mistake of not rallying to its defense. The outcome was Truman's election, a result so unexpected that one American newspaper found itself on the stands with the banner headline "Dewey Defeats Truman," which had been set in advance and released before the results were in. Truman had taken advantage of an important power of the presidency and had proved its effectiveness.

It must be stressed, however, that this power does not always operate with full efficacy. There are occasions when a president's voice can be subordinated to the voices of others—and Truman, paradoxically, again provides the best example. These are occasions of great danger to the American people because they usually occur when society is subject to heavy strains and authority is on the verge of breaking down. The most recent such moment in our history was the return in 1951 of General Douglas MacArthur from Japan after he had been removed from his command by Truman.

This was an instance in which a well-known rule of communications was demonstrated in its clearest form. Mechanical means of amplifying the voice and a command over all of the media are of no avail if the audience will not listen. At this crucial moment in American history, Truman had as many public-relations resources at his disposal as any other president up to that time. The radio networks and the then relatively feeble TV networks were his at any time he chose. Newspapers would accord him as much space as they could make available. But the American people did not want to listen.

The president had lost the most vital of all the elements in presidential authority—public confidence. It had gradually eroded under a series of political mistakes that Harry S Truman, as a senator, would never have made. A series of petty scandals—none of them of any magnitude and none of them involving the personal integrity of this unusually upright man—had made him look small and tinged with a murky variety of partisanship. Statements he had made in defense of victims of the congressional Red scare had been so poorly phrased that he appeared to be defending Communists and communism. And he had not been able to explain the highly subtle concept of the Korean War, a war in which the objective was not victory but merely the containment of aggression.

In this turbulent context, General MacArthur appeared as a white knight in shining armor. His orotund, rolling phrases were fuzzy in meaning, but they resounded with a grandiloquence that stirred the blood of a people who wanted to feel nobility of purpose in life. His bearing was that of a haughty, aloof aristocrat, the antithesis of the American democratic ideal, but his freshly pressed uniforms were obviously unspattered by the muck of ward politics. He was greeted with an evangelical fervor which, in retrospect, is difficult to credit by those who were not present in the worshipping throngs that greeted his thundering procession through the United States. When he spoke, people shouted and cheered as though they were hearing the words of John the Baptist. And when, at the conclusion of an address to Congress, he recited the words of a mawkish barracks-room ballad, "Old soldiers never die, they simply fade away," men and women sobbed as though they were listening to a sermon straight from the Mount.

The Administration was silent. It was helpless to dampen the ecstasy and the fervor. It feared, not without justification, that a demand by MacArthur for the reins of government would be received with a roaring "yes" from tens of millions of American throats. The situation was desperate. MacArthur was insisting on military action that could easily escalate the Korean War into World War III. The people were in no mood to listen to explanations. The situation was saved only by the heroic efforts of politically wise senators who ordered an investigation into the whole MacArthur episode, and chose to head it the master political craftsman of the twentieth century, Richard B. Russell of Georgia. Russell, whose unusual mind combined the political craftiness of a nineteenth-century Tammany leader with the culture and breadth of an Oxford don, perceived the only possible solution: Let MacArthur talk himself out before a congressional committee and then launch weeks of "high-level" hearings in which all the technical aspects of Asian military policy could be discussed in classroom fashion. The hearings ended with advocates of all points of view congratulating Russell for his objectivity and fairness and with MacArthur "fading away"—this time genuinely so—into obscurity. A year later, when MacArthur addressed the Republican national convention, a reporter for a major newspaper chain noted only that he did not look so grand in civilian clothing and that the klieg lights shining on his head revealed bald spots that were not discernible in the days of his military glory. He had been forgotten, but only because the arena of debate had been moved into the back room where the steam could be released gradually.

One is hard-pressed to think of a comparable situation since the rise of electronic communications media. Democratic strategists will never forget the powerful impact of Eisenhower's TV speeches on the farm bill in 1954 and the Landrum-Griffin Act of 1958, the details of which are no longer of general interest, but which were major partisan issues at the time. In thirty minutes, months of careful work were undone, and in the latter case an overwhelming Democratic congressional majority found itself helpless to stem a popular storm. The president had triumphed in areas of economic and social legislation where his qualifications to speak were almost nonexistent. In both cases, his logic was questionable. But it did not matter. No amount of political skill could offset the president's capacity to appeal to the nation at a time when the nation had confidence in him.

The third source of presidential power is his ability to place others in positions of authority or prestige. This is more than the power of appointment. A lawyer who is known to dine privately with the president (for example, Clark Clifford before he became Johnson's secretary of defense) is raised to a position of eminence in the legal profession. An author such as Truman Capote, who was seen frequently with President Kennedy's close associates and family, found that his readership increased overnight. A businessman such as banker Arthur Krim, who went to Camp David often with Lyndon Johnson, found his status in the business community enhanced. And all three are likely to use their newfound prestige to promote the cause of the president. By careful manipulation of such favors, a president can establish a network of Americans from coast to coast ready and anxious at any hour of the day or night to explain his cause, form supporting committees, or raise the money without which politics would be impossible. It may well be that an early sign in the decline of presidential power is the decline in the caliber of the people immediately around him.

All these powers added together are truly formidable. It is unlikely that any president could be defeated for reelection if he exercised them wisely. Franklin Roosevelt secured four terms in office, and it is not adequate to explain his dominance solely by the fact that he was a wartime president. He maintained a grip on reality and knew how to recover quickly from such mistakes as the Supreme Court packing bill. A president who suffers a defeat or a loss does so because he has made the wrong decisions and has not acted to recover from his errors.

The trend is clear. Over the passage of the years, what began as little more than managerial authority has become power over the life of the nation itself. The *right* to check this power still rests in Congress and the courts. But the *ability* to check assumes the capacity to offer alternatives, to explain them to the public, and to manage a structure that carries them out. In the modern age, when action with little time for reflection has become increasingly urgent, these capabilities are lessened with each passing day for every arm of the government except the presidency.

Underlying all these factors is the mechanism by which the chief executive has a monopoly on authoritative answers to crucial questions in a context of uncertainty. A president who defends and exploits his monopoly successfully is generally classified by historians as "strong." A president who permits this monopoly to be breached and allows others to dictate his response to important events is usually classified as "weak." In fact, most presidents represent a mixture of the two qualities.

Maintaining a monopoly of authoritative answers is the essence of leadership in any field. But the president has some unusual advantages that accrue to no one else. Some of these advantages flow from stated responsibilities that are clear, definite, and precise and recur year after year—such as the State of the Union message and the presentation of the budget, which set the stage for both political and governmental activity for the year. Others flow from the fact that he is the only person who has managerial control over the instruments with which a nation must respond to the crucial issues of life and death—the diplomatic services, the armed forces, the treasury, federal public works, police agencies, etc. Were all these instrumentalities to be exploited with proper skill, it is doubtful that any president could be removed from office except through death or senility. In actual practice, however, no president has sufficient wisdom or vitality to come up always with the proper answer at the proper time and in the proper place. Franklin Roosevelt's capacity to recover from his mistakes was not shared by many of his successors or predecessors. Sooner or later, every president either responds incorrectly or fails to respond at all, and it is probable that failure to respond at all is even more deadly to his leadership than failure to respond correctly.

The exercise of leadership has little or nothing to do with a president's personal popularity. Among the responses that a president should seek to invoke from the people, liking is probably the least important. (I am not referring to the president's psychological comfort but only to his capacity to lead.) No president has ever been more beloved by the American people than Dwight D. Eisenhower. He entered office on a tidal wave of enthusiasm.

His image was a combination of father, grandfather, and kindly uncle. He could do no wrong—so much so that even the revelation of a noisome scandal involving his closest personal adviser did not shake public esteem for him in the slightest. And yet no president since Warren Harding permitted the powers of leadership to be taken from him on so many occasions.

It is instructive to examine one of the most striking instances, one that illustrates how a president can lose his power to control events almost completely even though he does not sink in personal popularity. On October 4, 1957, the Soviet Union launched into outer space the first man-made satellite, Sputnik I. The announcement of the successful venture hit the people of the United States like a brick through a plate-glass window, shattering into tiny slivers the American illusion of technical superiority over the Soviet Union and creating fears and apprehensions greater even than those which had been produced by the armed might of the Axis powers in World War II. These apprehensions reached almost a fever pitch when less than a month later—November 3, 1957—a second Sputnik was successfully placed in orbit, this one carrying a live dog as a passenger. It was only a question of time until space vessels orbiting the earth would carry men and women far beyond the range of any conventional antiaircraft weapons. Americans found themselves confronted with the deadliest of all fears—fear of helplessness before the unknown.

The event had not been entirely unheralded. A few years earlier, Eisenhower had announced at a press conference that the U.S. was starting a project to place a man-made satellite in orbit around the earth. The announcement attracted little more than passing attention. It had been explained that the satellite would be only about the size of a basketball and its purpose would be scientific research. To a generation largely untrained in the laws of physics (and this is a safe generalization about the post–World War II generation) it was little more than a curiosity, a scientific stunt that seemed something of an anticlimax following the atomic and hydrogen bombs.

The actual presence of a Soviet satellite orbiting overhead was a different matter altogether. To the feverish imagination of people unaware of the limitations of technology, it opened up limitless vistas of hideous nightmares. It was assumed that in a short time the satellites would become space stations from which atomic bombs could be dropped on the United States without any prospects of defense. People imagined Soviet spies with superpowerful binoculars ferreting out the most cherished secrets of our country. Without knowing how it could be done, the "man on the street" assumed that control of the space around the earth meant control of the earth itself. And if there was one thing of which Americans were certain in the fall of 1957, it was that they did not want the earth controlled by the Soviet Union.

The discussion and the debate, unfortunately, took place at parties, at social gatherings, in bars, in private clubs. It quickly became apparent that the Administration was content to let it stay at that level. From the White House emerged only a few soothing words intimating that Sputnik and Muttnik, as they were popularly known, were merely scientific toys. President Eisenhower and his advisers were absorbed in balancing the budget and had no stomach for launching an outer-space program that obviously would cost billions of dollars and throw out the window the concepts of fiscal soundness so dear to the hearts of the "strong men" in the government—Secretary of Treasury George Humphrey and Presidential Assistant Sherman Adams. In their desire to keep things on an even keel, they neglected the most powerful instrument available to channel public discussion into rational forms—the presidential monopoly on authoritative answers.

It did not take long for another political figure to perceive the breach and rush in with political troops to seize and occupy a strong position. The Senate Democratic leader, Lyndon Johnson, had a platform from which he could operate—the Senate Armed Services Preparedness Subcommittee. It wasn't a very potent platform in comparison to the White House. But the White House platform wasn't being used at all, and by the time the Administration strategists became aware of what was happening to them, it was too late. Johnson had seized control of America's share of outer space and appeared to have elevated himself to the role of the chief—in fact the only—antagonist to Soviet domination of outer-space science.

The Senate Armed Services Preparedness Subcommittee had been little more than a caretaker operation since Johnson, its first chairman, had relinquished control of it to Senator Styles Bridges following the Republican election triumph of 1952. He had resumed the chairmanship in 1955 in addition to his majority leadership, but his preoccupation with running the Senate left him with little time to attend to the subcommittee's operation. Fundamentally, it was only a means of providing payroll for extra staff. Suddenly it was revitalized. Members of his personal staff on the Senate Democratic Policy Committee found themselves working full time on the Preparedness Subcommittee investigation of the outer-space program, and Edwin L. Weisl, one of the nation's most influential lawyers, was brought down from New York to direct the inquiries. The Senate caucus room became the center of national attention as scientist after scientist appeared on the witness stand to tell the subcommittee members (and, through television, the entire nation) of the marvels of outer space. The first witness, Edward Teller, the key physicist in developing the hydrogen bomb, was perfectly in tune with the thesis that control of outer space meant control of the earth. He ventured the hypothesis that the Sputnik was the first step in a process that ultimately would mean control of the weather and would place in the hands of one nation the ability to deny rainfall to another nation and turn the latter into a barren desert. Other scientists were somewhat more cautious. A few even suggested something that sounded in the time and circumstances like heresy—that exploration of the ocean depths was more important than outer space. The cautionary notes went unheeded. The American people wanted authoritative answers and if they did not come from their president, they were going to take them from the only people who offered them—Lyndon Johnson and the members and staff of the Senate Preparedness Subcommittee.

The Administration further weakened its position by inept efforts to pooh-pooh the subcommittee's inquiry. Sherman Adams allegedly referred to the investigation as "outer-space basketball." Word leaked from the White

House that Eisenhower had remarked to some friends, "Let Lyndon Johnson keep his head in the clouds. I am going to keep my feet on the ground." These observations ran so contrary to the mood of the American people that, to the extent they were noticed at all, they were merely offensive. The picture was that of a president ignoring what many people regarded as the greatest crisis in centuries while the Senate Democratic leader was working night and day to mobilize the nation to meet the challenge.

The hearings brought into full public view what had previously been only hinted at by columnists, the back-stage discussion about the feasibility of the intercontinental ballistic missile, which allegedly could hurl atomic bombs at the United States from the Soviet Union with the speed of a rifle bullet. In retrospect it is difficult, even for people who participated in the subcommittee inquiry, to be certain of some of the conclusions that were then drawn in good faith and with a sense of absolute certainty. But it was clear that the Soviet Union had leapfrogged the United States in the development of rocketry and therefore it was assumed that the Soviets were superior in the field of ICBMs. After five years of a Republican administration, there was little doubt as to the doorstep upon which the blame would be laid.

The situation reached a climax in January 1958, when Lyndon Johnson in addressing the routine Senate Democratic caucus that is held at the beginning of every session, delivered a speech of compelling power. It was widely described as the "Lyndon Johnson State of the Union Address." It is easy to see now that the speech was extravagant and overstated the situation confronting the American people. It was criticized by some Democrats (especially Eleanor Roosevelt) for its belligerent, somewhat martial tone. Eisenhower reacted, with justification, as though an act of lese majesty had been committed. But these reactions had little impact (although a few days later Johnson counterposed to the criticisms a suggestion that the development of outer-space exploration proceed under the aegis of the United Nations). The speech fitted into the public mood. The American people felt that their pride had been injured and their security threatened by the unprecedented Soviet triumph. They were willing to listen to a man who told them that they faced perils and had to react vigorously to salvage national prestige. The Space Act that followed was almost totally the work of Johnson and his staff—one of the few examples in the last fifty years of a major statute originating on Capitol Hill rather than in the White House. Eisenhower succeeded only in securing the adoption of a few minor amendments.

The picture of vigorous action on the part of the Democratic congressional leadership, as contrasted to inaction on the part of the Republican executive, unquestionably played a major role in the Democratic triumphs at the polls in the fall of 1958. The contrast was highlighted by a similar reaction to the recession of 1958, when Lyndon Johnson successfully urged highway, public works, and housing programs to create employment and tugged along in his wake a reluctant Eisenhower.

Between the two men, there was no doubt as to who was more popular. It was President Eisenhower. Nor was there any doubt as to who, for the time being, appeared to be leading the country. It was Senator Johnson. The presidential powers had been usurped, to some degree, without any violation whatsoever of the Constitution and the laws. Eisenhower had made one fatal mistake: He had not protected what should be the presidential monopoly on authoritative answers to crucial questions in a context of uncertainty. His popularity had not been harmed in the slightest, and within a few years Johnson's role in outer-space development was all but forgotten although the boost it had given to his national status persisted. Eisenhower's ability to govern had, however, been severely damaged and was not recovered until 1959 when, aroused by the Democratic electoral triumphs, he began exercising the powers of the presidency, especially through the veto. The Democratic leadership of Congress then found itself less able to dominate the national scene, even though its legislative majorities that year were larger.

The Democratic triumph in originating and enacting an outer-space statute was, of course, highly unusual. It was not repeated, except to a far lesser degree in the antirecession legislation of 1958—measures to step up public works and highway construction and stimulate home building. Nevertheless, throughout the eight years of the Eisenhower administration, it was clear—even during the two years the Republicans had a majority in the House and Senate—that in political expertise the Democratic leadership of Congress had the upper hand.

To those of us who had some association with the "loyal opposition," the ease with which the Republican administration could be outmaneuvered was astonishing. There were, naturally, certain limitations to what could be done. For example, we had to start with bills sent to Congress by the president (except for the instance of outer space). But once the bills arrived, it was only a matter of time until they were overhauled and converted into laws that clearly bore the label "Democratic"—and that then usually secured a presidential blessing. Public housing was not only preserved but enhanced. Appropriations for health research were doubled and even tripled with monotonous consistency. Social security was expanded against the heated opposition of the White House. Antimonopoly amendments were written into legislation to provide for commercial development of atomic energy. In eight years, only two clear-cut victories of magnitude were won by the Republicans when the battle was clearly joined—the adoption of flexible farm price supports and passage of the Landrum-Griffin bill to regulate labor-union health and welfare funds.

The formula was simple. It involved a careful analysis of the divisions within the two parties; a calculation of the most extreme Democratic objective that could be achieved on the basis of those divisions; the drafting of amendments calculated to unite the Democrats and divide the Republicans; and an obstinate refusal to fight for unattainable objectives. There were forces at work in the Senate and the House that made these tactics highly successful. President Eisenhower could not afford head-on collisions with the Democratic legislators because he had needed their support to achieve his foreign-policy objectives, most of which were unpalatable to many members of his own party. Southern Democrats, who normally could be expected to vote with the Republicans, were more amenable to supporting the Texas leadership of Lyndon Johnson and House Speaker Sam Rayburn—particularly as the belief grew in their ranks that a successful Johnson bid for the presidency was within the realm of possibility. Finally, the Republican leadership of both houses consisted of men who had played prominent roles in the anti-Eisenhower wing of their party and, though they were men of integrity, their hearts were not dedicated to crusading for their president.

The Democratic legislative triumphs were impressive indeed, but they are now largely forgotten and, in retrospect, this is understandable. The one thing that the Democratic leadership, for all its unquestioned superiority in political tactics, could not do was to make a serious dent in the prestige of Dwight Eisenhower. He concluded his second term as beloved by the American people as he had been on his inauguration day. And the Democrats promptly proceeded to nominate as his successor John Kennedy, a senator who had played virtually no legislative role other than to supply a vote for the string of victories.

The forces that led to the Kennedy presidential nomination over Johnson in 1960 are too complex (and too irrelevant to this book) to be discussed here. But the forces that sustained the high popularity of a president who was politically inept by every test except success at the polls, are very much to the point. Eisenhower's popularity cannot be doubted. Only once in his eight years did he fall below the 50 percent mark—to 49 percent in April 1958, in the midst of widespread unemployment and following his loss of leadership on the outer-space issue. Four months later the same poll showed him at 58 percent, and when he left office in January 1961, he was at 59 percent. And no practical politician doubts for a moment that the only barrier to a third term, had he so desired, was the constitutional two-term limitation imposed, ironically, by the Republican-controlled Eightieth Congress.

It is risky to speculate on the mood of a nation under any circumstances, but certain characteristics of the Eisenhower regime may suggest an answer. The most important is that no man who has held the office since George Washington was better equipped to fill the role of the president as chief of state than Dwight David Eisenhower. He had dignity. He had warmth. He was a man of apparent good will. He sincerely believed in the validity of America's symbols and he had an almost touching faith in the capacity of "right reasoning" to solve even the most complex problems. His lack of political expertise represented the traditional American concept of politics as a grubby business in which he was uninterested, rather than a lack of intelligence. All in all, it would be difficult to find a better man to preside over a nation. He was a king without arrogance, a potentate with a distaste for power, a moralist with no touch of fanaticism. The American people could regard him with a respect and affection that they did not accord even to Franklin Roosevelt, who had led them out of the Depression wilderness and through the largest war in recorded history. Nobody could really hate Eisenhower (although Democratic partisans and right-wing hysterics tried) but they could, and did, hate Roosevelt. The basic difference was probably FDR's expertise, which enabled him to rub salt into the wounds of his opponents time after time—an opportunity he did not forgo.

As a constitutional monarch, or a president under a parliamentary system, Ike could have had a lifetime job. And, in fact, Eisenhower's organizational methods bore some resemblance to constitutional monarchy. He himself, by all accounts, paid little attention to the day-to-day details of government. This was the business of men like George Humphrey, Secretary of State John Foster Dulles, Secretary of Defense Charles Wilson, Sherman Adams, and Jim Haggerty. He insisted that problems be resolved within the government itself and that the few that could not be winnowed out at lower levels be brought to him as one-page memorandums to which he could say "yes" or "no." When he made a speech, it was obviously a "speech from the throne" representing the views of "the government" rather than "the president."

To Democratic partisans, this whole process was little short of incomprehensible. We could not understand a man in a position of power who would not use the instruments of power available to him. The Democratic opposition was clever, sophisticated, and clear-eyed as to its goals, but it failed to take into account the folk wisdom that frequently rejects cleverness as trickery and political expertise as insincerity. One of the great tragedies of the Democratic party is that years later it still has not mastered this lesson.

In Dwight D. Eisenhower, the American people found an answer to their deep yearning for a presiding officer over their affairs. They did not care about his lack of expertise because they recognized instinctively that expertise can always be hired. They were looking for a symbol of legitimacy, continuity, and morality; and perhaps they were right in elevating these qualities to a position higher than the manipulative skill that resolves problems. It is possible that in reviewing the Eisenhower administration, we are looking at a blueprint for the future of the presidency.

Chapter VI

The American Versailles

THE MONARCHICAL CHARACTER of the White House was not apparent prior to the 1930's simply because it was a palace without a court. The building served primarily as living quarters for the First Family, and its successful operation required nothing except one or two secretaries and a staff of competent servants for entertaining. Under most administrations, the butler was probably more important than the people who were detailed to help the president with his official duties. After all, the preparation of a menu for a state banquet is more taxing on intellectual faculties than the maintenance of a presidential calendar and the bringing to him the papers and letters for his signature.

The government was managed largely through the departments that had been established by act of Congress. All of them were under the president's control, as Abraham Lincoln demonstrated when he refused the request by members of his cabinet that he allow them to run things during the Civil War. Before the Civil Service was instituted, the president could legally step into any agency and hire or fire without any constraints other than the normal considerations of politics. Nevertheless, governmental agencies—even in the "to the victor belong the spoils" era—tend to bureaucratize themselves. It is in their nature to respond to administrative rather than political exigencies. They will do what the president tells them to do but the performance will be reluctant and lacking in initiative whenever the demands made on them require striking out in new paths. They are instruments that the president can use, but they are not *his* instruments in the sense of courtiers in a palace.

All of the great monarchs of history learned early the necessity of having at their disposal a force beholden only to themselves and cut off from the rest of society. Sir Thomas Malory seems to have missed the true significance of King Arthur's Round Table. As long as his knights ate at it every day under King Arthur's watchful eye and lived in his palace where he could call them by shouting through the corridors, they were his to ensure that the kingdom would be ruled the way he wanted it ruled. Louis XIV did not build the Palace of Versailles as a tourist attraction but as a huge dormitory where he could keep tabs on the nobles who were disposed to become insubordinate if they spent all their time on their own estates. Peter the Great downgraded the boyars whose power rested on their distance from Moscow and brought the reins of government into his own hands by making all the top officials dependent on him. And the Turkish sultans reached the ultimate in the creation of personal force by raising young Christian boys captured in combat as Janissaries who lived solely to defend the ruler.

In a divided powers government, the examples set by Arthur, Louis, Peter, and the Porte are not feasible. A few close friends may be brought into the White House— Colonel House, for example, advising Woodrow Wilson. But this is usually little more than a hand-holding operation. When it comes to action, all presidents have to operate through Cabinet secretaries. This problem (it will always seem to be a problem to monarchs) was finally solved by Franklin Roosevelt. He persuaded Congress that he needed "expert" help, assistants "with a passion for anonymity." The request was granted, albeit with some reluctance by a Congress that sensed something amiss, because of his emphasis on expertise. Had he staffed the positions suddenly made available to him with older men and women, it might not have made so much difference. They would have served their terms in the psychological sense of taking a tour of duty and then returned to their former lives. The essence of the New Deal assistants under Roosevelt, however, was youth. The Corcorans, Cohens, Youngmans, Rowes, and Pritchards were still malleable—barely out of school. They were energetic, brilliant, resourceful, and dynamic. But they were also immature. To them, life began in the White House where the alpha and omega of existence was the successful execution of the orders that came down from the "chief."

There is a dramatic difference between the daily lives of White House assistants and the lives of aides in Congress or the executive agencies. In Congress, assistants' lives center around the man or woman for whom they work. They are forced, however, to brush up daily against the political constraints of their principals, an experience that tends to keep one close to social reality. People in the executive agencies are sheltered from political forces but have clear-cut tasks and know their position in the hierarchy. There are comprehensible measuring sticks by which they can judge their own performance. In the White House, too, there are shelters from political constraints but these jobs do not have clearly defined roles. The status of a White House assistant is measured by his proximity to the president—and he must gain that status himself, by scrambling to climb over the heads that are between him and the top man. The more assistants, the greater the Palace Guard infighting that ensues.

The White House staff has an inner political life of its

own. It consists of people who do not have fixed responsibilities—except in the rare instance of a President Eisenhower who brought to the mansion the staff and command organization of the army and imposed it with relentless and unyielding determination. The mere fact, however, that Eisenhower could do this demonstrates the basic character of the staff. It is the creature of the president, a group of people who have one purpose in life and one purpose only—to perform personal services for the man in charge.

This is essentially the life of the barnyard, as set forth so graphically in the study of the pecking order among chickens that every freshman sociology student must read. It is a question of who has the right to peck whom and who must submit to being pecked. There are only two important differences. The first is that in the barnyard the pecking order is determined by the individual strength and forcefulness of each chicken, whereas in the White House it depends on one's relationship to the barnyard keeper. Second, no one outside the barnyard glorifies the chickens and expects them to order the affairs of mankind. They are destined for the frying pan and that is that.

Since Franklin Roosevelt, the practice has increased of assigning titles and outlining, on paper at least, responsibilities for the members of the staff. Today, there is a press secretary, a special assistant for national security affairs, a special assistant for cabinet affairs, a special assistant for independent agencies, a special assistant for minorities, a special assistant for legislative liaison, and a special counsel. Many of the titles have little substance behind them. The special counsel during my tenure did almost no real legal work; for legal opinions the White House leaned on the executive agencies, especially the Justice Department. In two administrations, the special counsels were primarily speech writers (Theodore Sorensen and Harry McPherson), and although both were men of high legal competence, their opinions on points of law were rarely sought or offered. It was open knowledge, not only in the White House but to the Washington community at large, that their ability to put on paper sentences that would parse grammatically was the key to their position in the hierarchy.

To some extent, of course, the titles do have meaning. In these few cases, it is only because there are some functions in the White House that require an institutionalized approach and comprise continuing responsibilities on a day-to-day basis. The special assistant for national security affairs, for example, generally does handle national security affairs. His clear-cut role rests not on his expertise in international relations but on the more mundane fact that he controls the flow of communications concerning them to the president. Henry Kissinger, a man of unusual ability, found quickly that this gave him enough leverage to become Nixon's secretary of state. These communications are highly complex. They enter the White House in a bewildering flood. There must be routine procedures that pare them down to a point where they are digestible by the president. The administration of these procedures is a full-time job. Therefore, it follows that the person who holds it has the rare and cherished privilege in the White House of doing what he is supposed to do.

Another example of a position that has been institutionalized is that of the White House press secretary. But again, this is not due to the press secretary's expertise in handling the press, or, as it is more delicately termed, public relations. Public relations is actually the function of the president himself. Every president is his own press secretary (and this is probably reflected in the nature of the relations between the press and the presidents—it is something like being one's own lawyer). The press secretary has a series of routine duties that must be attended to by a full-time assistant. They are very unglamorous duties—chartering airplanes so the press can follow the president (the press, not the taxpayer, pays for the airplane); arranging hotel accommodations, notifying telegraph and telephone companies when extra facilities will be needed; arranging with police departments for special credentials for the press as the president travels about the country; dealing with the television networks as to where cameras can be placed. Without these arrangements, there could be no adequate coverage of a president. These duties are sufficiently exhausting, and require a sufficient degree of continuity, that it is impossible to allocate the responsibilities among a number of assistants to be performed on an ad hoc basis. Jim Haggerty was the only press secretary in the history of the White House who actually performed the job in accordance with the popular concept—dealing with and administering press policy. But he was able to do so only because Eisenhower was rigidly determined to delegate every administrative detail.

For other White House assistants there is only one fixed goal in life—somehow to gain and maintain access to the president. This process resembles nothing else known in the world except possibly the Japanese game of *go*, a contest in which there are very few fixed rules and the playing consists of laying down alternating counters in patterns that permit flexibility but seek to deny that flexibility to the opponent. The success of the player depends on the whim of the president. Consequently, the president's psychology is studied minutely, and a working day in the White House is marked by innumerable probes to determine which routes to the Oval Room are open and which end in a blind alley.

The techniques are astonishingly simple and require not subtlety but a willingness to test human credulity to its outermost limits. Basically, the methodology is to be present either personally or by a proxy piece of paper when "good news" arrives and to be certain that someone else is present when the news is bad. The battle-wise assistant develops to its highest degree the faculty of maintaining physical proximity coupled with the ability to disappear (by ducking down a hallway or stepping behind a post) at the right moments. The White House is architecturally well adapted to such tactics, since there are plenty of hallways and a plethora of concealing pillars.

When a president is happy and pleased, his assistants race behind him shoulder to shoulder in lockstep as he strides from the West Wing to the family quarters. When storm signals are flying, because of a "bad" column or an insulting statement by a foreign leader, the president makes the journey alone, watched only by the unblinking eyes of the Secret Service and the uniformed police who guard the Mansion.

The written word is crucial. But it is important that memorandums reach the president at the "right" moment, and this is something no assistant can manage personally. There is a traditional approach, however, that never fails. The way to a man's heart may be through his stomach but the best path to his favorable attention usually lies through his secretary—especially if she is endowed with the age-old feminine faculty of measuring masculine emotional temperature with precision. The assistant so fortunate as to have a secretary who rooms with that secretary has won three-quarters of the battle. It is even conceivable that his suggestions will go to the top of the stack while others are rerouted without even receiving presidential attention.

The question of physical proximity in terms of office space is a primary cause of battle. The favored position in the past was the West Wing, which housed the special counsel, the national security council staff, the legislative liaison staff, the press secretary, the special assistant for cabinet affairs, and the appointments secretary. An office in the East Wing automatically relegated its possessor to the status of "resident intellectual"—someone who was useful as window dressing when academic meetings were being held but who was not to be entrusted with the important business of the nation. An assignment to the Executive Office Building was banishment to the outer darkness of the technical world, made up of people who were "useful" and well informed but who did not have the ear of the president and therefore did not participate in what is euphemistically called "making policy." Subsequent presidents have changed the geographical locations but it is a safe bet that the essential nature of the struggle for position remains unchanged.

It is vital to the White House assistant that he receive a constant flow of information on the mood of the president and the latest problems that are occupying his attention. Since the assistant himself cannot be in more than one place at a time and since he cannot be too obvious in his search for intelligence, he himself must have an assistant—preferably one who is young, ambitious, hyperthyroid, and possessed of an excellent pair of feet. A considerable amount of the motion that characterizes the White House is due to the restless prowling of the assistants to the assistants, and a courtier is well advised not to leave his office empty with imprudent papers on his desk. If he does, he may suffer the major penalty of indiscretion—an unexpectedly sharp remark from the president or, worse, the expounding of one of his cherished ideas by another.

The only aspect of "palace-guard" politics that requires subtlety is the use of the press. The inexperienced courtier may make the mistake of using his press contacts (which it takes a positive effort of will not to acquire) to secure favorable mention of his name in public. But the wilier practitioners of the art of palace knife-fighting take a different tack. They seek to feature their competitors' names in a context that will displease the man who holds the real power. This reverse-thrust technique is more complex than it appears on first glance. It is not inconceivable, for example, that a newspaper story speculating on the promotion of an assistant to higher office may be the death knell of that assistant's governmental career. It all depends on the psychology of the president, but whatever that psychology, there will always be people around him who are willing to play it for whatever it is worth.

It is a stultifying business, and history prepares us poorly for the realities of palace intrigue. Somehow, in the studies of monarchies, the intrigants loom larger than life—men and women of titanic, though evil, proportions—and the intrigues appear as fiendishly cunning, intricate, and complex plots. It comes as a shock to discover that the principals are small-bore and the plots themselves dreary.

The sensitive mind boggles at the revelation that the empty-headed girl with the Betty Boop pout and the vacant stare, idly painting her fingernails alongside an IBM typewriter, is a twentieth-century Nell Gwyn, or that the neatly groomed youth with the choirboy face, spouting the liturgical clichés of the behavioral sciences, is Rasputin with a haircut. Even more shattering psychologically is the realization that the assistant who shows up at the bedchamber at 7:15 in the morning with a Gallup poll demonstrating a five-point rise in popularity is displaying the total sum of the *court* wisdom of a Richelieu (who, of course, had other forms of wisdom as well), or that the absurdly posturing young man who is careful to present a secretary with frilly lingerie at Christmas is following in the footsteps of Potemkin. History, in this respect, has let us down badly—not by telling us that virtue always conquers evil but by painting pedestrian activities in exciting colors.

The White House assistant must learn that his enemy is not towering evil but boring inanity. If he is to survive, he must drop his preconceived notions and get down to the proper level. It is one thing to battle Grendel, another to grapple with Sammy Glick. Either can be handled by employment of the appropriate tactics. But Grendel is at least predictable—he fights in the field with club and sword. It is only Glick who appears disconcertingly at the banquet table in the castle armed with the deadlier weapons of flattery and piety. The life of a courtier is to be Sammy Glick or to fight Sammy Glick— and all of his sisters and his uncles and his cousins and his aunts. Sammy has the edge because he cares more about the prize.

The most desired position, the one that symbolizes ultimate triumph, is attendance in the morning when the president awakens, rested and ready to transact business. To occupy this position, no sacrifice is too great. An assistant will arise at three or four in the morning and hustle down to the White House looking for an excuse to dash over to the mansion with a memorandum. If he is successful, he can return to the West Wing with the ultimate symbol of success—the mission of relaying to the other assistants the presidential decisions and orders for the day. If he can succeed in fulfilling this function for several days in a row, he becomes known as "the most influential man in the White House" and his triumph is complete.

This title, incidentally, may be bestowed on one person in the privacy of the Mansion and on a different person in the public press. No one who has ever worked in the White House can escape a feeling of skepticism when he reads accounts of the relative positions in the hierarchy of special assistants.

The problem is twofold—the reaction of the system on

the assistants themselves, and the reaction of the system on the presidents. There is good reason to believe that it is unhealthy in either case.

It is an exhausting life, but there is solace along Embassy Row and in Georgetown drawing rooms. The presidential assistant, wearied from a long day with the knife, can find ample diversion any night of the week. He may feast on couscous at the Saudi Arabian Embassy, sip champagne with the French, or plump delicate mini-tamales into his mouth among the Mexicans. There is always some action somewhere in town, and he has the added advantage of not needing an invitation. Doors open automatically for him, and he can step into any party to the fluttering and flattering attention of the hostess and whatever society writers have been assigned to the event. At least once in his tenure he will dine tête-à-tête with the Soviet ambassador and his wife in a small room where the atmosphere is intimate and the food is served family style.

Of course, there is a penalty to be paid for taking advantage of these ever-beckoning diversions. There are presidents who do work nights (following an afternoon nap), and a person's position in the pecking order can easily be shifted by his presence or absence at a crucial moment when a prompt explanation may satisfy presidential curiosity or assuage presidential wrath. Every assistant knows that no matter what hour he leaves the building someone will still be there with access to a presidential "hot line," even if it is only the duty officer in the situation room (referred to by adepts as the "sit" room).

A White House assistant lives a life of anxiety. There is no fixed point in his daily routine, other than the occasional smile of approbation or nod of approval that comes from the president. He is denied the inner comfort of a man who has a specific task to perform and who is measured by professional standards as to whether he has performed the task well or poorly. He may be aware of the fact that his performance on any specific assignment may be good, even superb in objective terms. But this is of no importance if there is a failure of appreciation on the part of his chief. Therefore, except for highly unusual men, the goal is not to perform superbly but to perform spectacularly. The two aims are not always compatible.

There is a tendency on the part of assistants to bring to the White House problems that should not properly be there, frequently to the disadvantage of the president. In the 1960's, for example, far too many labor disputes were brought within the gates to receive the personal attention of the president. There are times, of course, when a dispute raises issues so perilous to the health and safety of the United States that such action is justified. This can be said of the railroad strike in 1964. But there is reason to believe that neither the steel strike of 1965 nor the maritime strike of 1966 should have been so treated. Both were settled successfully, but they merely paved the way for bringing into the White House the airline strike of 1966 that resulted in a disastrous setback to Lyndon Johnson. It is doubtful that he would have taken over this dispute had he not been surrounded by assistants whose eyes were fixed on the possibility of a spectacular announcement rather than on the long-range trends in labor-management relations that made it impossible to achieve a settlement by executive intervention.

From the president's standpoint, the greatest staff problem is that of maintaining his contact with the reality that lies outside the White House walls. Very few have succeeded in doing so. They start their administrations fresh from the political wars, which have a tendency to keep men closely tied to the facts of life, but it is only a matter of time until the White House assistants close in like a praetorian guard. Since they are the only people other than his family a president sees every day, they become to him the voice of the people. They are the closest he has to outside contacts, and it is inevitable that he comes to regard them as humanity itself.

Even the vision of so earthy a politician as Lyndon Johnson became blurred as the years went by. He mistook the alert, taut, well-groomed young men around him for "American youth" and could never comprehend the origins of the long-haired, slovenly attired youngsters who hooted at him so savagely when he traveled (and eventually made most travel impossible) and who raged and stormed outside the White House gates. To him, they appeared to be extraterrestrial invaders—not only non-American but nonearthly. Certainly, they did not fit the pattern of young men and women whom he had assembled so painstakingly and who were so obviously, in his eyes, the embodiment of the nation's dream.

The president who resisted this temptation most strongly, and who maintained his political skill longest, was Franklin Roosevelt. He understood thoroughly the weaknesses of the staff system in the White House. He saw to it that under no circumstances could the people in his immediate vicinity control his access to information. Every staff assistant from the New Deal days recalls the experience of bringing a report to FDR and discovering, in the course of the conversation, that the president had gained from some mysterious, outside source knowledge of aspects of the project of which the assistant himself was unaware. None of Roosevelt's assistants, with the possible exception of Harry Hopkins, ever felt that his position was secure. And none of them would have dared to withhold any information. The penalties were too swift and too sure to permit what would anyway have been a futile exercise.

It is difficult, however, for a president to maintain sources of information outside his immediate staff. It requires a positive effort of will. This situation arises from the general nature of the presidency.

For many years, a corporation sold a popular mouthwash to the American people on the basis that it would inhibit bad breath. The slogan under which the product was merchandised—"Even your best friends won't tell you"—meant that the subject was too delicate to mention and that a person could exude the foulest odors without being aware of the fact. As far as the mouthwash was concerned, the slogan was somewhat misleading—not only your best friends but your worst enemies will tell you if you have bad breath. But the concept that "even your best friends won't tell you" about unpleasant things applies with tremendous force to the president.

As noted, an essential characteristic of monarchy is untouchability. No one touches a king unless he is specifically invited to do so. No one thrusts unpleasant thoughts upon a king unless he is ordered to do so, and even then he does so at his own peril. The response to unpleasant information has been fixed by a pattern with a long history. Every courtier recalls, either literally or instinctively, what happened to the messenger who brought Peter the Great the news of the Russian defeat by Charles XII at the Battle of Narva. The courtier was strangled by decree of the czar. A modern-day monarch—at least a monarch in the White House—cannot direct the placing of a noose around a messenger's throat for bringing him bad news. But his frown can mean social and economic strangulation. Only a very brave or a very foolish person will suffer that frown.

Furthermore, an outsider has a sense of diffidence in approaching a president to tell him "the facts of life" about his staff. It is in the same class as telling a father about the shortcomings of his son. The only people who do it are boors, whose opinion is little valued under the best of circumstances. Consequently, a president can go through an entire term without knowing that some of his most trusted assistants have created resentments that have undermined his political position. He will, of course, read occasional newspaper articles describing the activities. But he is bound to regard them as attacks by a jealous opposition, and the effect on his thinking will be the reverse of what was intended.

A "strong" president, if strength is defined as determination to have one's own way, paradoxically is more liable to suffer from the operations of the White House staff system than one who is "weak." The strong man has a propensity to create an environment to his liking and to weed out ruthlessly those assistants who might persist in presenting him with irritating thoughts. It is no accident that White House staffs under the regime of a forceful president tend to become more and more colorless and more and more nondescript as time goes on. Palace-guard survivors learn early to camouflage themselves with a coating of battleship gray.

The "weak" president, on the other hand, is more susceptible to conflicting currents and less ready to eliminate strong-minded people from his immediate vicinity. The mere fact that he is somewhat "wishy-washy" at least assures that he will keep open some avenues of approach and that the courtier who has been cast out may find a way back in.

I have a feeling that Camelot was not a very happy place. Even the gentle language of Malory does not fully cloak hints of intrigue, corruption, and distrust—reaching as high as Guinevere. And the "Table Round" seems better adapted to boozing in a vain effort to drown disappointment than to knightly discourse on chivalrous deeds and weighty matters of state.

In fact, Malory makes virtually no effort to describe Camelot as a seat of government. King Arthur was presumably beloved by his subjects because he was wise and valiant. But how did he handle road building, public charity, or the administration of justice? Such questions had to wait several hundred years for the advent of Mark Twain, whose entirely fictitious (and wholly irreverent) account was probably much closer to the reality than that produced by the original sources.

It is this aspect that gives cause for concern. The psychological ease of those who reside in Camelot does not matter except to the individuals themselves. But the type of government that Camelot produces affects every individual and, ultimately, can determine the character of the society in which we all must live.

Chapter VII

The End of the Party Line

ONE OF THE more unfortunate developments of the past thirty years is the disappearance of the political party as a factor in the political life of the nation. There are still remnants of once-powerful political machines in Chicago and a few West Coast areas. But on the whole, political parties have been reduced to the function of paring down the number of candidates for office so that the voters can choose between two people when they go to the polls at the general election. This is a useful role, as our system is not adapted to digest a multiplicity of candidates. It does not, however, serve to moderate the more extreme varieties of action in government, nor does it help in keeping political leaders in touch with reality.

Actually, America's political parties have been ideological in the European sense for very few years in our history. They were founded as the outcome of historical events and then went through a long period of evolution in which they shook off most of their intellectual baggage to become mechanisms for the election of people who would continue to preserve the mechanism for further electing at the next election. The Democratic party is the oldest in name, but in name only. If one strips away the rhetoric about Jefferson and Jackson and looks at the party the way it is today, it is obvious that it is the enfeebled descendant of the coalition established by Franklin Roosevelt—northern labor, southern and western agriculture, intellectuals, and ethnic groups. The Republican party speaks of itself as the party of Abraham Lincoln. But if one looks at it as it is today, it is obviously a haven for the so-called yuppies—the upwardly mobile middle class of the mid-twentieth century produced by the technology and economics of the mid-twentieth century. The New England and midwestern farmers who were the backbone of Lincoln's party are now only trace elements.

It is interesting to refer to the preceding paragraph and note that a meaningful definition of either party must come in terms of constituencies rather than political principles. Since the days of Franklin Roosevelt, people who call themselves conservatives have tended to flock to the Republican party and people who call themselves liberals have tended to flock to the Democratic party. But in each instance, they tend to remain nothing but a troublesome faction. When I am pressed for a quick description of the differences between the two parties, the best I can do is to say that the Republicans have trouble with right-wing crackpots and the Democrats have trouble with left-wing crackpots. To go beyond that, however, and define the two parties as conservative or liberal is to exercise one's imagination beyond permissible limits. It is not at all difficult to find Republicans who are far more liberal than any Democrat or Democrats who are far more conservative than any Republican.

There was a period in which one could designate the Republican party as the party of "sound money" and the Democratic party as the party of low interest rates. Even then, the ideologies were not too important. At bottom, both of the parties were highly pragmatic and, as such, they served as a balance wheel on the political and governmental scene. Politicians needed them to get elected and therefore they at least listened to cautionary admonitions from the "bosses." It was well that they did so. The machines that ran the two parties tended to be corrupt, crass, and closed against any inspiring vision of the future. They were also in intimate contact with the voters and they were thinking in terms of the general election in the fall rather than in terms of registering political biases in the primary. They knew how to head off the nomination of extremists who would guarantee a lost race when the real chips were down.

There are many reasons why the political parties lost their influence. The most important is probably a complicated set of circumstances that separated them from the governing process and left them with nothing but electioneering. Their demise does not fill very many people with regret. Nevertheless, when they went, they took with them something of great value—a communication link between the ordinary citizen and the top of the governing pyramid. It has not been replaced adequately. As late as 1944, Democratic party leaders could persuade Franklin Roosevelt to abandon his desire to nominate Henry Wallace for a second term and replace him with Harry Truman. But the last political leader who could get any presidential ear was Richard Daley, whose Chicago machine did not survive his death.

All of this means that another door to social reality is closed as far as presidents are concerned. The political parties served as a link between political leaders and social reality because they were connected to the governing process (as dispensers of patronage) and, at the same time, had a form of independence from the people in office. Presidents come and presidents go, but the Kellys, the Nashes, the Hagues, the Crumps, and Tammany stay on forever—or so it once seemed. Two things brought their dynasties to an end. First, various forms of civil service spread through communities and patronage lost its importance. Second, without patronage they were unable to maintain their independent status and become creatures of the men and women in office. To visit either the Republican or the Democratic National Committee in the modern era is to be exposed solely to talk about fund-raising—to pay off the debts of the last convention and to finance the next convention. All they can really do is provide an arena for the selection of a coalition candidate for the presidency. In recent years, the conventions have been so cut and dried due to the increase in binding primaries that even that function has been weakened.

As far as the party that does not control the White House, this is a situation of chaos. Its officials plod along toward the next convention with an occasional effort to find speakers out of Congress to reply to the president. As far as the party that controls the White House is concerned, it belongs to the president. It is his to do with as he sees fit—to use it, abuse it, or ignore it altogether. He appoints the national chairman, dominates the national committee, and determines the extent and character of its activities. Members of the national staff come to see him, hat in hand, in no mood to raise perplexing and troublesome questions. And he can, if he so desires, appoint assistants who will count every postage stamp used by that staff.

This situation arises primarily out of the basic nature of the American political party. It is not an ideological instrument nor does it have "members," in the European sense of the word. It is purely a technical convenience. There is no genuine inner party life between conventions at the national level except for the jockeyings of a few partisan bureaucrats to attain some degree of proximity to the president. When a party is out of power, the jockeying becomes more interesting. It still goes on through frantic efforts to become close to the "leader." Since no one can identify this person with certainty, it is something like playing blindfold chess with no one calling off the opponent's moves or announcing "check" and "checkmate."

Traditionally, the American political party has been held in very low esteem, except by newly arrived immigrant groups who have found in their ward leaders the only sympathetic help available to guide them in bewildering circumstances. A few of the higher offices, such as national committeeman, are sought by "respectable" citizens—chiefly because they involve at least one presidential reception a year. But generally, "politics" has been regarded as something in which a "gentleman" does not engage. It has been a domain reserved for the very crass or the very young whose elders assume that they will get over their idealistic fling and engage in more acceptable pursuits.

The result has been an increasing tendency to stray outside the party machinery for political assistance even in campaign years. Most presidents look to "citizens' committees" and "scientists' committees" plus a host of others with a "nonpartisan" tinge as their most effective political aids. Partially this trend is due to restrictive campaign laws, which make a proliferation of committees essential for fund-raising purposes. But even more important, it reflects a feeling that many citizens are repelled by a political party. They want their presidents to be untouched by the muck of partisanship.

Presidents are probably correct in their judgment on the efficacy of nonpartisan election machinery. It is an excellent source of otherwise unobtainable votes, and people campaigning for office tend to hold such sources in very high regard. Unfortunately for parties, this means that a successful candidate is unlikely to regard the party machinery as something to which he should pay much attention after he is in office. It did not appear to him crucial during the campaign (presidents are usually con-

vinced that they won their elections single-handed anyway) and it appears irrelevant to the high problems of
statecraft that enter the Executive Mansion so intoxicat-
ingly. It is not even replaced by the solemn nonpartisan
committees composed of distinguished citizens that fold
up as soon as they have paid off their debts.

This status is dimly sensed by the groups of young
people who are urging so vehemently what they call "the
politics of participation." They feel that there should be
some kind of yeasty ferment in daily political life, something other than a chance to blow horns, pop balloons,
and strain larynxes every four years. They are right, but
they are not going to get it through "party reform."
What is needed is basic change in the presidency itself,
and this is not going to come through the action of the
national committees. The inner political life is not going
to be yeasty so long as the people in power do not have
to listen. There will be no participatory politics as long as
a president can so easily separate himself from the partisan process.

A closely related problem has been raised by a few
academicians. There have been few subjects more hotly
discussed among political scientists in the past thirty years
than that of "party responsibility." But, with a few notable exceptions, the bulk of the discussion has ignored the
determining factor in whether it is possible to have "responsible" political parties at all—the office of the
presidency.

The framework of government is a group of appropriate channels through which power relationships can be
exercised. The art of politics is the effort to seize and
occupy key positions in that framework. Therefore, it
would seem to be a truism that the limits of legal political
activity within a society are established by the framework
of government. But this elementary truism has apparently
made no impact on the political thinking of some acade-

micians. They still assume that the character of political parties can be determined by conscious acts of will, that a group of people can form a party of predetermined character and use it as a vehicle for securing power. This is an oversimplified view, but one that has dominated political discussion and has rarely been examined.

It is necessary to define the term "responsible" political party for the discussion to have any meaning. As the term is used among students of government, it means an ideological party—one whose platform can be read in the secure knowledge that if the party achieves power it will act, or try to act, according to the planks that have been set forth.

The United States has had many such parties in the course of its political history. There have been the Populist party, the Greenback party, the Socialist party, the Socialist Labor party, the Communist party, the Prohibition party, and a number of others too numerous to have achieved more than a footnote in erudite studies of the political process. Some of these parties secured widespread popular support for a brief period. But they all disappeared, either by absorption into one of the major parties or simply by lapsing into limbo. The more successful, such as the Farmer-Labor party in Minnesota or the Progressive party in Wisconsin, succeeded in making a formal alliance with either the Democrats or the Republicans. Others, such as the Socialist party, converted themselves into discussion groups. One, the Liberal party of New York, has managed to survive, but only as a broker of convenience offering voters a simplified method of splitting their tickets.

Party reformers have treated the inability of these parties to survive as a reflection of mental aberration on the part of the electorate. They have assumed that there is a demand for such parties and that the only issue is to find the set of ideological proposals with sufficient appeal to put one of those parties into power. What they have ignored is a fundamental reality of the American political structure that permits the continued existence of two parties, and two parties only.

This reality is the inability of the executive branch to form a coalition. The Constitution of the United States lodges *all* executive authority in the hands of one man and there is no form of human ingenuity that can transform one man into a coalition.

This factor is basic and determining. Democratic government is inconceivable except through a coalition. There are too many different approaches to every issue to permit any one point of view to hold more than a fleeting majority. Stable government can be achieved only through the processes of accommodation. When a form of government specifically prohibits such an accommodation from being made, the inevitable necessity of coalition requires that the accommodation be at another level. It is for this reason that America's major political parties are essentially coalitions—and can only be coalitions.

For many years, professional politicians found themselves embarrassed on any college campus by a simple request for a definition of the differences between the two parties. The question should not truly have been embarrassing, because it was based upon a false premise— that America's political parties resembled the ideological groupings of Europe. The professional politicians made the mistake of accepting the premise and on that basis they were lost. They could resort only to generalities about the "party of progress" or the "party of stability"— generalities not very impressive to youthful minds that have not yet fallen into the mental ruts that sometimes go with maturity. The professionals left the question shrouded in mystery.

In so doing, they performed a disservice to the American political system by making it look ridiculous. It is not ridiculous, although I feel intensely that some very fundamental changes are necessary. It is a logical system that reacts to the necessities of the power relationships in our society. And one of these reactions is the coalition political party.

The party platform is an outstanding example of a rational activity by a coalition party, which has been condemned as futile by academicians because of their failure to understand fundamental premises. It is usually damned as an expression of pious generalities that has no purpose other than to mislead the electorate with sugar-coated promises—and that generally fails to achieve even that purpose. Political commentators emphasize throughout a campaign that the presidential candidates are paying little or no attention to the platform and will pay even less attention to it in the event that they are elected. This latter criticism is accurate but irrelevant. It is irrelevant because it assumes that the purpose of a party platform is to tell the voters what the party will do once it is in power. Nothing could be farther from reality. The true purpose of a party platform is to determine the outer limits under which the coalition can be held together, and the intense fighting that goes on at every party convention is a reflection of this purpose.

The party platform has served its purpose the moment it is adopted. It has provided the arena within which contending ideological factions have decided whether they will "stay in" or "walk out." This may seem a roundabout way of making that determination but it would be difficult to devise a better mechanism. The ruling hierarchy of a political party must somehow determine the price of maintaining unity and must pass judgment on whether that price is worth paying. There is no reliable guide other than to raise issues of gut and emotion and then watch the partisans as they negotiate acceptable language. Sometimes, as in the Democratic convention of 1948, the party decides that the price is too high and permits a walkout by some of the delegates. In this instance, it proved to be a wise decision and Truman went ahead to win the election. In 1912, however, the Republican party made a decision that the price of unity was too high and the resulting party split enabled the Democrats to elect Wilson, their second president since the Civil War. Regardless of the wisdom of either decision, the decision had to be made.

The necessity for coalition political parties is so obvious to the average professional politician that he is unable, as a general rule, even to engage in a rational dialogue on the subject with the reformers. Any such discussion—and a number have been held over the years—invariably erupts in a free-for-all. The professional politician understands instinctively the premises of the coalition party but is incapable of articulating them. The reformer understands the need for ideological parties but except in rare instances appears incapable of comprehending the necessary conditions for forming them. Someday, this gulf of understanding must be crossed so that the two groups can work together to devise a system that gives greater weight to ideology.

It is essential, in this connection, to distinguish between coalition government and bipartisanship. The concept of bipartisanship occupies a hallowed position in American political folklore, but its only practical effect has been to increase the strength of some presidents under some circumstances. The most revered part of the folklore is that of the bipartisan foreign policy. It is assumed that somehow politics should end "at the water's edge" and that U.S. foreign policy should reflect the will of *all* the people. This fantastic bit of nonsense (fantastic because it never has and never will be true) has been accepted only because the word "partisan" is pejorative in our vocabulary, and people shrink from applying it to crucial decisions. The Constitution of the United States gives the president exclusive control over foreign policy, subject only to certain checks. A president is, almost by definition, a political man. There is no rational basis for assuming that he is going to be bipartisan about fiscal policy, labor policy, farm policy, or any other issue on which differing views are possible. He may, of course, turn to members of the other party for advice on foreign affairs, but he is just as likely to turn to those members for advice on the other issues. Actually, there is no mechanism whatsoever in the American system whereby a policy of any kind can be made bipartisan, because our political parties cannot negotiate meaningful agreements on matters of substance. No one can state with certainty who officially represents a political party when it does not control the presidency. It is possible to deal with the congressional leaders of a minority party or with some of its governors. But none of them can "speak" for their party in any authoritative sense. The cold fact is that when a Democratic president consults Republicans, he is consulting them in their status as interested American citizens, or, at most, in their capacity as representatives of small groups of Republicans, and not as ideological representatives of the GOP.

So-called bipartisan government, as actually practiced in the United States, rests upon a grant of status to members of another party by a political leader who is in power. Sometimes it is wise for him to grant such status; sometimes it is unwise. But under either set of circumstances it is something he can do or undo by a conscious act of will. A true coalition, on the other hand, represents status that people can exact as a price for cooperation because of the political power at their command. If an Italian cabinet includes members of a minority party, it is because the members of the majority party do not have enough political power to form a government without the help of the minority. There isn't anything else that can be done.

Under the American constitutional system, there are no forces that can *compel* a president of the United States to allocate positions to members of the minority party in order to hang on to the presidency. The president represents the monopoly of ultimate, executive power. He serves by tenure and nothing short of the complicated procedures of impeachment, death, or resignation, or the Twenty-fifth Amendment can remove him from office. He keeps the reins of power in his hands even if his following in the country has shrunk to 10 percent or to zero. And if, as an act of political wisdom, he places minority members in his cabinet they enter as *his* agents, not the agents of their party. Their partisan affiliations have no more relevancy to their administration of office than their church affiliations or social ties.

A major example of this kind of bipartisanship came during World War II, when Franklin Roosevelt placed Republicans in his Cabinet—Henry L. Stimson and Frank Knox, Secretaries of War and Navy, respectively. It was a shrewd move by any standard. It nailed down the concept that the conduct of the war was an enterprise in which the president deserved the support of all of the people regardless of their attitude toward his politics. It disarmed opposition and gave Roosevelt elbow room that he would not otherwise have had. It was also an entirely safe move. Neither Stimson nor Knox represented the Republican party in the Roosevelt Cabinet any more than they represented the legal profession or newspaper publishing. They became solely agents of the president, administering key agencies under his personal direction and control. At the time of the appointments, many Republicans muttered (quite rightly) over what they regarded as a "trick" to disarm them as an opposition party. Stimson and Knox underwent considerable criticism from their fellow members of the GOP, but the criticism was muted. It was not politic to fault the president on what appeared to be a tremendous gesture of farsighted goodwill and bipartisanship.

Since that time, it has become commonplace for presidents to place members of the other party in their Cabinets. The gesture is so taken for granted that it scarcely causes the lift of an eyebrow or a ripple in the political community. There was even some perfunctory criticism of Richard Nixon for not naming a Democrat to his first Cabinet. The American people have adjusted to the idea, realizing that it does not represent a coalition in any true sense of the word and is known as bipartisanship only through a very loose use of the term.

The lack of clear-cut ideological parties is also stressed by the president's relationship to the Congress. The president does not "control" Congress at any time, not even at periods of great popularity when it is politic for most legislators to go along with him. His true relationship to Congress is that of a highly important factor that the legislators must take into account. When the president's popularity is immense, he represents the major factor and can get pretty much what he wants regardless of the political composition of either branch. As soon as his poll ratings start to slip, Congress reasserts its independence. The question of whether the president has a majority of his own party in the Congress is academic. What matters is whether his following on *both* sides of the legislative aisle constitutes a majority.

Harry Truman served as president for two full years with a Congress dominated by the opposite party. He managed to convince the public at the end of those two years that the Congress had been so obstructive that he was now entitled to a Democratic Congress as well as reelection. But a nonpartisan appraisal of the Eightieth (Republican) Congress will lead to the conclusion that it was much more productive than Truman ever admitted.

The Eightieth Congress forced into law the Taft-Hartley Labor Act and the two-term presidential limitation over Truman's objections. On the other hand it gave him the British aid bill, the Truman Doctrine (for Greece and Turkey), and the Marshall Plan. The latter, by any criteria, represented superior acts of statesmanship and a high degree of cooperation. The two Democratic Congresses that followed were far less cooperative and far less productive.

Dwight Eisenhower, as a Republican, served the last three-quarters of his presidency with Democratic Congresses and in the first quarter his Republican majority was of a hairline quality. Nevertheless, no one can maintain that he was blocked or frustrated in any important particular by the Democrats. Lyndon Johnson, the Democratic leader of the Senate during the Eisenhower administration, actually built his reputation as a national statesman by continuously putting congressional Republicans in an obstructive light and Eisenhower in a position to be rescued time and time again by Democrats from the machinations of his own party. It was a tactic that worked because it was valid. Democrats were much more sympathetic to Eisenhower than were the members of his own party.

The fact that the coalition system works among American political parties, however, is not sufficient reason to conclude that the coalition parties are ideal by any stretch of the imagination. They have been under heavy criticism from political scientists for many years and the criticisms are justified.

> They do not give Americans a sufficiently clear choice.
>
> They do not provide an outlet for large segments of the population, who feel excluded from the major parties.
>
> They reduce political discussion to a low level of pious generalities that ill prepare the American people for the problems that lie ahead.

In the 1968 campaign, for example, the only candidate who really discussed the issues that were moving the American people was the third-party representative, George Wallace. The fact that his discussion was the "wrong" discussion, that he was a dangerous demagogue arousing ugly emotions, must not obscure the fact that he had a virtual monopoly in talking about the things that counted. Both Richard Nixon and Hubert Humphrey debated questions on the basis of generalities and emotional appeals to past loyalties. They were wise to do so. They knew that coalition parties offered no adequate platform for pointed discussions. Wallace, on the other hand, labored under no such handicap. His own political platform had been created especially for him and he did not have to worry about any sizable group of people walking out. By the same token, he had no possibility of winning the election, because his fundamental approach was too divisive.

In the United States, true ideological discussion never takes place at the political-party level. Americans thresh out their ideological differences in other forums—labor unions, women's clubs, newspaper columns (including letters to the editor), in farm cooperatives, and other organizations that are not constrained by the necessity of holding together coalescing forces. It is assumed at a national convention that ideological problems have been aired before the delegates got anywhere near the place and that no minds are going to be changed by intellectual persuasion. The convention itself becomes an arena in which the ideological blocs can test their strength and determine what accommodations they must make in order to secure their maximum influence within the party.

This is the factor that has led to the elaborate "ticket balancing" that always characterizes the party team. A "liberal" Democrat is likely to name a more conservative vice-presidential candidate; a western Republican is likely to look east for his running mate. This has real value in terms of stressing national unity and helping the winning candidate start off with some hope of achieving a consensus. But it also leads all too frequently to the selection of admittedly inferior men over admittedly superior ones. The superior men are bypassed simply because they do not help to hold together the party coalition.

Perhaps the problems of ideological parties can best be seen by a look at Congress. On a number of occasions, minor parties have succeeded in electing representatives and senators. When I first began covering the nation's legislature as a newspaper reporter, the Senate included two members of the Farmer-Labor party, one member of the Progressive party, and one independent. The House contained a number of Farmer-Laborites and Progressives and one member of the American Labor party. All of them were, strictly speaking, a bloody nuisance to the officials of Congress charged with the housekeeping functions of that body. It was not possible to build separate cloakrooms for the minor-party members. Patronage problems were insuperable—how do you give a member of the American Labor party $\frac{1}{435}$th of a page?—and the Republican and Democratic leadership opened every Congress with an endless wrangle about how the minor-party members were to receive their committee assignments. These, of course, were all housekeeping problems, which only represented headaches. But there were also revealing of the fact that the American system is incapable of coping easily with more than two political parties—one in power and one in opposition.

None of this is to be construed as persuasive argument against ideological political groupings. In fact, there are increasing pressures for such groupings. The "McCarthyite" revolt in the Democratic party of 1968 represented a strong surge of people who were not ideologically satisfied with what remained of the coalition of Franklin

Roosevelt. The Republican presidential nomination of Barry Goldwater in 1964 was a successful effort of ideologically motivated people to find a political voice. Both efforts ended in electoral failure, in fact were doomed to failure even before they started. The objective of these political drives was the capture of executive power, which is held by one man. There was no constitutional way in which the ideologues of either the McCarthy or the Goldwater persuasion could obtain a measure of relief from their frustrations by securing some part of the executive power. The battle for the presidency is an all or nothing proposition, and the losers are left out in the cold for another four years. Unless executive power can somehow be dispersed through cabinet officials, under a system whereby they hold their positions because they have gained them through political struggle, ideological groupings will remain deprived of an adequate outlet.

The arguments for responsible party government are compelling. But their logic is irrelevant so long as the result of political activity is elevation to the presidency and so long as the president is a man with a complete monopoly of ultimate answers and with no direct responsibility to another elected body. Those who desire ideological politics must await the day when mechanisms are available that permit coalition at the government level, and thereby relieve our political parties of the necessity of filling this role. Even more important is that the job of keeping presidents in touch with reality—once performed by the political machines—is not going to be done until we devise parties with a degree of independence.

Chapter VIII

The Fourth Estate

OF ALL THE institutions of our society, the one that has the best potential for keeping presidents in touch with reality is the press. The fact that it does not do so is revealing of the nature of the position he occupies. It is not a failure of will or intent on the part of the journalists. It is rather the psychological defense mechanisms with which the White House supplies its occupants. And when it comes to the electronic press, presidents have found so many forms of control that it no longer has terrors to the political mind. Whatever comes over the air waves that is critical can easily be offset and turned into an asset.

In modern politics, the press plays a subdued role as contrasted to its conduct of just a few decades ago. Almost unnoticed, American journalism has ceased to be a real participant in the political struggles of the nation. It has become a recorder of deeds and a recorder of opinion. It is no longer an active force in the sense that such men as Joseph Pulitzer, E. W. Scripps, Roy Howard, William Randolph Hearst, Henry Luce, and Colonel Robert McCormick were a force. Those men had political power and they used it. They took part in the selection of candidates; in the strategy of campaigns; and in the conduct of government itself. As a result, they were consulted by politicians who actively sought their favor—not just for favorable news stories but for the strength they had in the political world.

That era has fairly well vanished and from the standpoint of the daily news diet available to the American people it is well that it did so. Even the *Chicago Tribune,* which once would not mention a Democrat unless he was found in a hayloft with a sheep, now presents a reasonably well-balanced account of the news. The other side of the coin, however, is that with few exceptions leading politicians no longer regard the press as a force with which they must come to terms. Where they once dealt with it as with other politicians, they now deal with it through professional public relations–type spokesmen.

This does not mean that critical reporting has been abandoned. The press can still be relied upon to search for malfeasance in government and expose it when it is found. It also carries contrasting political opinions in the form of columns by authors who are not on the newspaper payrolls and who therefore can be repudiated when they write something unpopular. All in all, it is an arm's-length process that does not have the impact that goes with face-to-face confrontation.

What may be even more important is the presidential discovery that television is a communications device made to order for the chief executive. Of all the developments of modern times, none has placed the president in a stronger position. He can go on the air when he wants to go on it; he can set up the background in an impressive aura that none of his opponents can equal; and, as Ronald Reagan has discovered, he can make points merely by waving at the camera as he walks to a helicopter on the south lawn of the White House. Most important, it allows him to take the offensive on almost any issue and leave his opponents where they can only react—a defensive position that never carries a debate.

Nevertheless, despite all these advantages, presidents

seem to consider the press a deadly enemy. That is unfortunate. From the standpoint of the president himself, the biggest advantage of the press is its unique status as the one form of communication that reaches him every day that is not shaped specifically for him. Virtually all other forms are shaped either directly or indirectly by people who wish either to conciliate or antagonize him. In either case, the contents of the message and the manner in which it is phrased are governed as much by the sender's judgment of how best to produce a desired effect on the recipient as by the substantive matters with which the sender deals.

Many newspaper reports and a much larger number of columns are written solely for their impact on the president. Newspaper reporters are not exempt from the universal urge to shape history, or even to curry favor with an important element in their livelihood. But the newspaper itself is addressed to the public. If it is to survive, it must, every day, offer a reasonable presentation of events with certain bounds of accuracy and perspective. It cannot dedicate itself solely to the edification of one man, no matter how important that man may be. And while it can rearrange facts or interpret them in the best or worst possible light, its ability to *change* facts is severely limited as long as any degree of competition remains.

Presidents have considerable leverage with which to manipulate part of the press, and all try to do so with varying degrees of success. The principal source of the leverage is the unusual position of the president as one of the very few figures in public life who has in his exclusive possession a type of news virtually indispensable to the social and economic security of any reporter assigned to cover the White House full time. This category of newsworthy material consists of the president himself—his thoughts, his relationship with his friends and employees, his routine habits, his personal likes and dislikes, his intimate moments with his family and associates. The fact that these things constitute "news" of a front-page variety gives the president a trading power with individual reporters of such magnitude that it must be seen at close quarters to be credited.

There is no other official of the government who can make a top headline story merely by releasing a routine list of his daily activities. There is no other official of the government who can be certain of universal newspaper play by merely releasing a picture of a quiet dinner with boyhood friends. There is no other official who can attract public attention merely by granting an interview consisting of reflections, no matter how banal or mundane, on social trends in fields where he has no expertise and in which his concepts are totally irrelevant to his function as a public servant.

It is not hard for any other high government official "to make news." But, with the exception of scandal, he can do so only through activities that bear a direct relationship to his official function. A secretary of state can command headlines by denouncing the Soviet Union; but no one cares about his views on dogs. A secretary of labor can inspire widespread interest by commenting on a nationwide strike; but only in his hometown is any newspaper likely to print a picture of him playing with his grandson. An attorney general receives respectful attention when he delivers an opinion on crime in the streets; but no reporter will be credited with an exclusive for revealing that he prefers Scotch to bourbon. As the interest of correspondents in government officials extends primarily to their *public* acts, it is not possible for those officials to monopolize the release of their activities. Consequently, the press can approach them on a basis of independence that cannot be sustained by those who cover the president. It is not at all unusual for newspapers to assign correspondents to cover cabinet agencies who are personally at odds with the heads of the agencies, but any responsible editor will have long second thoughts before assigning to the White House a man or a woman who has personally incurred presidential wrath or even the dislike of secretaries in the press office. Sometimes, long second thoughts will result in the assignment of the offending reporter anyway. But such occasions are rare.

The temptations inherent in this situation to "trade out"—to swap golden nuggets for "good" stories—are so overwhelming that few, if any, presidents of the modern era have been able to resist. It is taken for granted in the Washington press corps that there are certain "favorite" reporters who have "an in with the old man." It is impossible for this state of affairs to be concealed for any length of time. The press corps, in the early days of any administration, watches nervously for the first story that begins "the president is known to feel" or "the president has told close associates." There is a constant jockeying for a position that will permit a correspondent to deliver to his paper a set of exclusive photographs of the president and the First Lady walking in the White House garden (pictures taken by the official White House photographer). And the competition among the television networks for exclusive film reaches heights of savagery.

Any president would be well advised to resist the opportunities that are held forth so temptingly. Many presidents have been so advised, but it is not yet recorded that the advice has been accepted. The rewards of "trading out" are immediate and apparent. The penalties, which follow inexorably, are far down the road—so far down, in fact, that when they are exacted, it is difficult to trace back their origins. Every president who has played favorites has suffered in the long run. It is doubtful that any of them will ever accept the truth of that statement. To understand it, it is necessary to back up for a moment and analyze the problem of presidential press relations.

A president's press problems are really quite simple. He does not have to make any extraordinary effort to attract attention. All channels of public communication are open to him any hour of the day or night. Every word that he utters will, sooner or later, find its way into print. If he does not like the paraphrases used by the newspaper reporters, he can take to the airwaves and the electronic media will deliver his exact language, with his own intonations, into every American home. He can keep reporters at his side twenty-four hours a day, if he so chooses, and he can depend on their rapt attention to his every word. There is no other human being on the face of the globe who has comparable facilities for projecting every thought, every nuance, that is in his mind.

Theodore Roosevelt considered the White House "a bully pulpit," and more than fifty years later an assistant wrote the phrase into a speech by Lyndon Johnson. It is likely that left to his own devices Johnson would have thought in terms of a magnificent stage—and the transition from pulpit to stage is one of the more significant trends in modern history.

A pulpit is a platform for persuasion and exhortation. A stage is a setting for a presentation that may or may not carry a message. It can be an instrument for education and leadership or an attention-getting device for entertainment.

As a stage, the White House has no equal in the electronic age. It is equipped with props that cannot be matched by Hollywood, Broadway, and Madison Avenue combined. It is staffed by technicians capable of solving the most difficult electronics problems in the wink of an eye. Above all, it commands the instant and total attention of television networks, which dominate the largest audience in all history.

In no other field is the power of a president so immediately apparent as in his relationship with the television networks. His slightest wish is treated as an imperial ukase, and no press secretary ever has to ask for time on the air. He need indicate only that the president will be available.

During the Johnson administration the networks went so far as to staff a highly expensive TV room in the White House with warm cameras manned throughout the working day. This gave the president the potential of appearing live on nationwide networks at a few minutes' notice, and the fact that he used the facility only rarely did not deter television executives from meeting high weekly bills for its operation.

Presented with instrumentalities like this, the average public-relations man planning an industrial or political campaign would, with justification, consider himself in seventh heaven. He would regard as absolutely ludicrous an assertion that he had a "press problem" (although he might be tempted to leave this impression with his client). And he would be correct. The reality is that a president has no press problems (except for a few minor administrative technicalities), but he does have political problems, all of which are reflected in their most acute form by the press.

Why, then, do presidents spend so much time discussing with their confidants—and sometimes with the public—their "press problems"? Why, then, have the relationships between presidents and the press over the years traveled such a rocky road? The answer involves some complicated and subtle points that no one comprehends completely but that are worthy of study not just in terms of the press but in terms of the presidency itself.

There is a deep-seated human tendency to confuse unhappy news with unhappy events and to assume that if the news can be altered, so can the events. This tendency is particularly accentuated among monarchs. Peter the Great strangled the courier who brought him the tidings of his defeat at Narva. John Kennedy (or at least someone on his staff) canceled the White House subscription to the *New York Herald Tribune,* which had consistently been critical of him. The two acts differed only in the degree of retaliation available to the two men.

At stake is a twentieth-century form of the word magic of primitive society. There is a widespread predisposition to assume that the qualities that words represent can somehow be transferred to objects, regardless of their content. Thus, the advertising man holds, as an article of faith, that any stale idea will become exciting if the word "exciting" is drummed into the human consciousness a sufficient number of times by the electronic media. And similarly, it is assumed that a man somehow becomes dedicated and forward looking if he can persuade people to associate the two adjectives with his name in print.

The techniques of word magic are unquestionably successful when they are applied to commodities that are necessities of life and that do not differ essentially from competing commodities, such as soap. Whether they apply in a more sophisticated environment is questionable. And whether they can override objective facts is something that has yet to be demonstrated. A president deals in objective facts. If the nation is at war, he must draft young men to risk their lives in battle. If the nation embarks on great projects, he must tax the people in order to finance the federal activities. When he makes the promises that all political leaders make in moments of euphoria, he arouses expectations that will not be quieted except through fulfillment.

It is only in George Orwell's world that war can be labeled peace, brutality labeled justice, economic misery labeled prosperity. Within the White House itself it is possible to apply much of the Orwellian formula with a high degree of success. No assistant or secretary has yet won an argument with a president—and very few have tried. It is entirely possible within the walls of 1600 Pennsylvania Avenue to create a universe that is utterly to the liking of the principal occupant. He will not go so far as to alter all facts. But he can be certain that the facts will be brought to him in the most sympathetic form and with the harshest blows softened. Within this atmosphere, the only grating note comes from the newspapers and the electronic media, which are produced on the outside and are not subject to rewriting. The *Congressional Record* and the White House record can be "corrected"—but not, at least at present, the record of the Fourth Estate.

Unfortunately for the mental peace of presidents, events cannot be altered significantly by control over the printed word, at least not for any extended period of time. Although the White House does have at its own command instrumentalities for manipulating the press, they are effective only in regard to adjectives, not to the hard, substantive news that is the ultimate shaper of public opinion. Furthermore, the more successful the manipulation, the less useful becomes that part of the press which has been manipulated.

This situation arises out of the principal communications problem that faces every president—maintaining believability. The very factors that give the chief executive his tremendous advantage in the field of public relations also give him his greatest problem. It is simply that he is covered around the clock, his every word taken down and filed somewhere. Consequently, he is under the compulsion—if he is to be believed—to make his actions fit his words. Both his words and his actions make an extremely deep impression. He can lose the confidence of the people very quickly when the two do not coincide.

Until Ronald Reagan, a president was subjected to rules and tests that did not apply to other elected officials, for reasons I will discuss later. A senator could announce his ringing support of law and order in the streets of our cities without any fear of embarrassment over the future trend of crime statistics. But a president who made the same statement had to follow it up with action against muggers, thieves, and rapists and if the crime statistics did not go down, he was in trouble. A governor could take a firm stand on cleaning up air pollution, and if the atmosphere remained foul he could explain to his constituents that the cause was the noisome discharge of sulphur-laden smoke from across the state line and there was nothing he could do about it. But a president who assumed a similar stance could never convince the American people that the problem was beyond his control.

In assessing a president, there has always been a deeply ingrained public assumption that his choices are determined by what he wants to do and what he does not want to do, and he is, quite rightly, not accorded the benefit of the doubt when reality fails to measure up to his predictions. This is a very harsh test indeed, but there is a simple answer—presidents need not open their mouths until they have thought their way through the problem and devised workable solutions for which they need not apologize. It will be a great day for the country if this ever becomes the rule, but that day will never arrive.

Idle words are a luxury in which no president can indulge. Every presidential inauguration is preceded by a campaign in which the promises are, at the very least, extravagant. Fortunately, the beginning of a term is marked by public willingness to give the new president every opportunity, and if he uses this "honeymoon period" to establish his credibility, he can look forward to a relatively secure eight-year tenure in office.

The classic story of the gap between promise and performance goes back to the political grand master Franklin Roosevelt. In the 1932 campaign he promised the American people that he would cut governmental spending and balance the budget—a foolish promise that was forgotten almost immediately after the New Dealers entered Washington, frantic in their desire to deliver some relief to the Depression-stricken populace. A torrent of spending measures spewed out of the Capitol in the famous "100 Days" of FDR. Republicans, as soon as they recovered from their shock over the magnitude of their defeat, launched a campaign to remind Roosevelt publicly of his promises to cut spending. The principal promise had been made in a speech in Pittsburgh, and after a few days of particularly vehement GOP attack, Roosevelt called in his adviser Judge Samuel Rosenman and asked him to study the speech and produce an explanation. Rosenman returned in a matter of hours and said: "Mr. President, there is only one way to explain this speech. Deny that you ever made it!"

Fortunately, Roosevelt was still in the honeymoon period and the problems confronting the American people were so great that no one really cared about budget cutting. He was never again, however, granted such leeway, and he quickly learned to match words with action and to forgo promises, or at least make them so fuzzy that they were incomprehensible, when he lacked the resources to back them. As has been stated many times in this book, Mr. Roosevelt was a remarkable man who learned even from his own mistakes. This is one trait that few of his predecessors or his successors emulated.

The influence of a president is so great that people very soon identify those who are known as his "spokesmen." He eventually finds thoughts and programs attributed to him solely because they appeared in the articles of "pet" newspaper writers. When such journalists move to his defense in print, their explanations of his actions are suspect and discounted by presidential observers.

It is dangerous for newspaper reporters to have close friendships with political leaders. Such unfortunates find themselves identified as "sycophants" regardless of how scrupulous they are in handling their contacts. One of the outstanding examples was the columnist William S. White, a man of massive integrity, whose fortunes declined under the Johnson administration simply because of a friendship with the president that dated back more than thirty-five years. White, whose politics were far more conservative than those of the president, found that he could not write as forcefully as he wished on many subjects without embarrassing the White House because his words were interpreted as emanating from the Oval Room. His circulation actually picked up when Johnson left the White House, because people started to read him for what *he* was saying rather than for what they thought the *president* was saying, and he had a natural audience for his point of view.

Even more important, since manipulation of the press involves favoritism to some reporters it inevitably creates antagonism among others. There is an old political rule: "Every time a man does a favor he makes nineteen enemies and one ingrate." Obviously, favors cannot be done for every member of the press or they become meaningless. For every reporter who is placed in an advantageous position, several others must be placed in disadvantageous positions. Every president who plays the game inevitably winds up with more enemies than friends.

Basically, however, the long-standing antagonism between presidents and the press has deeper roots than the childish game that the White House usually plays with the Washington press corps. It is more validly traced to the fundamental dichotomy of interest that exists between journalists and politicians. No amount of manipulation can ever produce newspapers that are satisfactory to political leaders, or politicians who are satisfactory to journalists (unless George Orwell's nightmare, in which politicians had the capacity not only to produce newspapers but to rewrite the newspapers of the past, comes to fruition). A few words are necessary to this point.

Politicians as a class are dedicated to changing the world. With very few exceptions, they have in their minds some bright and shining ideal that is so obviously superior to what exists that it seems to be reality, with the actual world around them merely some kind of an aberration. Journalists, on the other hand, are held, to some degree, to the facts. They can play with adjectives; they can arrange the facts in any order that suits their convenience; they can give their prejudices full sway. But it is still their mission to present the world as it is. The two points of view are fundamentally incompatible.

Since the politician is oriented toward changing the world, he is constantly in a search for help. He divides the people with whom he must deal into friend or foe—those who have a "constructive" attitude and those who are purely "aginners." To have any force and effect as a political leader, he must be a partisan. And no partisan ever seized and maintained a position of power on the basis of self-examination and inner doubts. An Adlai Stevenson could arouse the respect and admiration of millions of people, but, like Hamlet who never became king, he never became president and it is doubtful that there is any conceivable set of circumstances under which he would ever have achieved the prize.

It is an article of faith with most politicians that any newspaper item even remotely touching on the government was written through partisan inspiration, not just because it happened. The concept that there are professional standards that determine news leads and news placement is alien to their view of society.

In justice, it must be recognized that a large proportion of political stories originate with a choice morsel leaked to the press for a partisan purpose. The Washington reporter who does not play off Democrats and Republicans against each other is simply ignoring a fundamental tool of his trade and is not destined for success. An occasional plug in return for a hot item is considered within the bounds of ethical conduct.

But the politician's view of the press is not limited to recognition of this obvious aspect of the game. He does not concede that there are events that will find their way into newspapers without any partisan help whatsoever. Moreover, he is incapable of crediting reporters with the ability to make simple deductions unassisted by people with an ax to grind.

An illustrative incident that stays vividly in my mind took place in the late 1940's, when I was a reporter for the United Press. The Democrats had just recaptured Congress after two years of Republican domination and the interregnum had produced some interesting shifts in the Democratic hierarchy. Among other things, the inexorable workings of the seniority system had placed Representative William L. Dawson of Illinois in the top spot on the House Executive Expenditures Committee. Since Dawson was the first black to be in this position since Reconstruction, this was news by any standard, particularly as the committee had broad investigative powers. Furthermore, there were a number of southern members in the group.

A poll of the committee was practically a reflex action. My first call was to a southern congressman. My question was simply whether there would be any trouble. The response was a snarl: "When did [some name unknown to me] reach you?" I was taken aback—even more so when I discovered that the congressman, with whom I had reasonably cordial relations, was referring to a small-town lawyer who was building an opposition political machine in his district. He accepted my statement that I had never heard of his foe but remained unshaken in his conviction that someone had "told" me there would be trouble or I would not have phoned him. His conviction was reinforced later in the day when he was called with the identical query by members of other wire services and newspapers. This, to him, was proof of conspiracy, not simply evidence that professional journalists were reacting to a professional standard of judgment. (It should be added that the committee poll disclosed no opposition to Dawson and the stories that were written merely stated that he would become chairman.)

Few politicians do not cherish privately the notion that there should be some regulation of the news. To most of them, "freedom of the press" is a gigantic put-on, a clever ploy that has enabled publishers as an economic group in our society to conduct themselves with a degree of arrogance and disregard of the public interest that is denied to other groups. The "ploy" has succeeded to an extent where it cannot be challenged publicly and therefore must be accorded formal deference. But the deference is purely formal and rarely expressed with heartfelt enthusiasm.

If censorship ever comes to the United States, it will explode out of the frustrations of a political leader convinced that the public good is being thwarted by self-serving reporters distorting the news. It will be the culmination of the natural political instinct to extend to the press the same standards he applies to the rest of society—does this help or hurt a worthy cause? The crusader is more likely to sound the death knell of free expression than the cynic.

The great game of politics is a highly personal pursuit in which official activity and social amenities are inextricably intermingled. A politician really does not expect a fellow human being to sell his soul for a handshake or a free barbecue. But he is always hurt and bewildered when the recipient of the shake or the beef responds in a mood that he interprets as antagonistic. This attitude is extended not only to other politicians but to business executives, professionals, clerics, and the press. It is impossible for journalists—even those who are psychologically disposed to walk in the footsteps of the world's oldest profession—to respond on every occasion with what the political leader regards as an appropriately grateful reciprocity. Therefore, in the politician's mind newspaper reporters are invariably guilty of ingratitude. Furthermore, politicians look to members of the press to be "constructive," to help them put across worthwhile programs for the betterment of humanity. It should be added, in all justice, that this is strikingly similar to the attitude of civic leaders, who begin every crusade for municipal betterment by calling on the editor of the local newspaper and asking him to "get behind" it.

The concept of a "constructive reporter" is a contradiction in terms. A reporter who selects stories on the basis of "the national interest" is actually doing the national interest a disservice. He has no business making such decisions. The closest he can come to it and still remain true to his trade is to report what others conceive to be "in the national interest." This is a point that no successful politician can grasp.

Frequently, newspapers themselves fail to grasp the point. The classic case is the downplaying by *The New York Times* of the projected invasion of the Bay of Pigs in Cuba. Here was an instance where those who decided to temper the news were thoroughly convinced that they were acting in the national interest because if they featured the story, the invasion would have been called off. They did not feature the story, the invasion did take place, the result was a debacle because of inadequate planning, and American prestige dipped to a new low.

This, of course, will not serve in the slightest to convince future political leaders that newspapers should place reporting of the news ahead of what they consider to be "the national interest." It is impossible for them to think otherwise. The political leader who rises to the top moves through a world that is sharply delineated between those who are helping him, those who are opposing him, and those who are uncommitted but can be swung in any direction. His success has been based on the manipulation of these three groups to achieve what he regards as fulfillment of the national interest—and such manipulation is, in most instances, entirely legitimate. The whole political process would break down and democratic government would be impossible without the existence of people skilled in this art. To persuade them that the press should be an exception would be pushing their credulity beyond human limits.

Furthermore, the politician is a human being subject to the normal tendency to overgeneralize from his own experiences. He knows that some members of the press can be manipulated. Therefore, he assumes that those who resist his blandishments have simply been reached first by a competitor. He is consciously encouraged in this belief by the journalists who "play ball" with him.

The importance of a "source" can be measured not only by its news value but by the degree of its exclusivity. To maintain his position in his industry, a reporter must display professional competence in judging and presenting news. But to advance, he must also demonstrate a capacity to obtain information unavailable to others—or at least available only on a restricted or delayed basis. There are both positive and negative paths that can be followed in achieving this capacity, and the artful journalist is capable of following both courses.

The positive path is to persuade important newsmakers that they can have confidence in the manner in which the reporter will handle a story. The reporter presents himself as one who will not divulge off-the-record material, will not embarrass his informant by identifying his source, will not twist the facts to present an event in an unfavorable light. This approach is vital to a successful reporting career and is not to be disdained.

The negative path is consciously to feed the paranoia that characterizes virtually every politician to some degree. A few words of sympathy over the unfair treatment by the "eastern press" (or the liberal press or the conservative press) is an effective method of slamming doors against competitors. An important leader who can be persuaded that his journalistic "friend" is the lone holdout against a "press conspiracy" can serve as a meal ticket for many years.

Since the press as a whole cannot be won over by tactics that political leaders regard as legitimate, it is inevitable that journalists eventually become the "enemy." In addition, they become the personification of all the frustrating forces that make the life of a president so difficult. Therefore, over a period of time, it is certain that the political leader will vent his spleen against the press, not realizing that he is really venting his spleen against the whole intractable environment that surrounds him. It is an easy matter to find legitimate grounds for criticizing the press. It is less easy to realize that all these grounds apply to the world generally.

Every president has his collection of inaccuracies in press coverage and is willing to regale his listeners by recounting them for hours. Seen in perspective, these inaccuracies are usually trivial and reflect only the fact that reporters are human beings who are bound to make errors under the constant pressure of reporting world-shaking events almost as soon as they happen. An objective evaluation is that the degree of accuracy with which the news is reported is astounding when it is contrasted with the conditions under which it is gathered. But a politician smarting under the lash of public criticism is not very likely to be objective.

Every president has his horror stories of press arrogance. But press arrogance is merely a reflection of public arrogance. Almost every American feels qualified to give the president advice on the most complicated and subtle questions of economics, law, and international relations. It would be surprising if journalists were exempt from this universal temptation.

Every president can recite valid examples of press bias and is entitled legitimately to some sympathy for the manner in which he is treated by opposition newspapers. But the assumption that bias is a journalistic characteristic rather than a condition of humanity is a distorted view of the universe. When a person enters politics, he undertakes to deal with *all* human characteristics and it is not an acceptable alibi to cite some of them as overwhelming. If press bias were an absolute bar to political success, this nation would never have had an Abraham Lincoln, and Franklin D. Roosevelt and Harry S Truman would have been denied a second term.

A president's problem in dealing with the press is precisely the same as his problem in dealing with the public at large. But no president can find it within his ego to concede that he has failed in any degree with the public. It is far more satisfying to blame his failures on the press because his problems then can be attributed to a conspiracy. He can blame the "eastern press," the "Republican press," or the "liberal press." He then does not stand indicted within his own consciousness (the most terrible court of all) as having failed. He was the victim of vindictiveness on the part of a selfish group and he can attribute his failure to the meanness of others rather than to his own inadequacies.

Chapter IX

The One-Way Street

ONE OF THE most profound changes that has come to the presidency has resulted from a new factor in American life—assassination as a political instrument. It is not that assassination itself is new—three presidents were killed before John F. Kennedy—but that it has become a continuous presence that seems to be lurking behind every shadow.

In the past, it was incomprehensible to most Americans that assassination could become an everyday fear. It was a remote horror, distant even from the violence that was such an integral part of frontier life. For at least two generations, it was merely a part of "history," something that belonged in the same category as the murder of the two princes in the tower or the killing of Julius Caesar.

Whatever may have been the reaction at the time, the assassination of Abraham Lincoln appeared to many in the perspective of history to be almost an appropriate climax to the life of a great and tragic man. James Garfield's administration made so little impact on the overall stream of American consciousness that today he is known to most people only because he was killed—and nine out of ten in any gathering of reasonably well-educated Americans would be hard-pressed to name the assassin. It was not until the death of William McKinley at the beginning of this century that specific steps were taken against the American equivalent of regicide and the full-time job of protecting the president was assigned to the Street Service.

In retrospect, it is strange that there have not been more assassination attempts in American history. The president is one of the most tempting targets to twisted minds that has ever been established. To kill a president is to kill a nation and thereby reserve space in the halls of immortality—or at least ensure a permanent footnote in histories of the American republic. And, until World War I, the president was highly accessible. Carl Sandburg makes a number of references to the manner in which Lincoln encountered people with whom he did not have an appointment just on a stroll through the White House. Apparently it was an open institution with nothing sealed off except the family living quarters.

It is not an open institution now. Access is possible only to those with passes or appointments, with strict identification required both at the gate and inside the building. The tourists who throng the ceremonial part of the Mansion do so under the watchful eyes of guards who are as vigilant as they are pleasant. Every list of people invited to White House ceremonies or social affairs is carefully scanned and checked against government security files.

The careful control of entry to the White House, however, is not the process that has made such an impact on the presidency. It would be necessary under any circumstances. Otherwise the building would be so filled with visitors that work in it would become impossible. The more important aspect is the determined effort of all concerned to make the security arrangements of the White House portable, to wrap them around the president whenever he ventures outside the grounds.

Harry Truman was stretching things somewhat when he said that the Secret Service agent was the only man who could tell the president what to do. This is a type of hyperbole in which presidents, for some reason, glory (Lyndon Johnson was fond of telling everyone how his cook told him what to eat). But once the objectives of a presidential movement are set, the Secret Service pretty well has the last word on how the movement will be made, and for a group of men who are possessed of an unusually high degree of tact, they can be remarkably firm.

The rules are simple. Make trips as fast as possible. Avoid crowds wherever possible. Where crowds cannot be avoided (or where the president insists on them), have the people gathered where they can be controlled. Command every high platform. Stand ready at every moment to get between the president and anyone who might pose a threat.

During the early days of his administration, Lyndon Johnson balked at the rules of security. He had a deep emotional awareness of the importance of some form of physical contact between the president and the electorate. It was impossible for him to shake the hand of every living American citizen, but he was able to shake—or at least touch—the hands of thousands and he told me that he believed each one would go home and pass on the handshake to hundreds of others. "When I was a young man, I would have given several weeks' pay to shake the hand of a man who had shaken the hand of a president," he once said. "I don't believe people have changed much in that regard."

The result was virtual abolition of the security rules that governed not only travel but the White House itself. On a walk around the south grounds, he was apt to throw open the gates and admit fifty or sixty tourists to take the walk with him. A crowd at an airport was sure to find him in the very middle. If the people were behind a fence, he would pass rapidly down the line tapping their outstretched hands with both of his. (Members of the press worked up an irresistibly comic parody of the action with one correspondent standing behind another with his arms under the armpits of the front man. That way, four hands could be touched at the same time.)

The impulse to take his hand was so strong that some would actually tear into his skin. He cherished the experience. On his return to an airplane from a foray into a public gathering, the first necessity was to treat the wounds with antiseptic and then some kind of soothing ointment. He would dwell lovingly on each gash, describing in detail how it had happened. Listening to the conversation, however, did not produce the feeling of a masochist enjoying his pain. He obviously regarded the process as one of communion. Had he been more sophisticated in theology, I suspect he would have thought of the scars as stigmata from the Cross.

As his popularity waned with the accelerating tempo of the war in Vietnam, he became increasingly reclusive. As far as the Secret Service was concerned, this was a godsend. The agents were no longer faced by a president who was ready at all times to cancel any of their plans to reduce his vulnerability. The hatred that was building up against him dictated the higher degree of security. But with it went all of his zest for the job. He felt—and I believe he was right—that a president who could not reach out directly to the American people could not run the country.

Since Johnson left office, only one president has really tried to restore any direct contact with the masses. Jimmy Carter had some of the same populist roots as LBJ. His walk down Pennsylvania Avenue arm in arm with his wife on Inauguration Day was in the Johnson tradition. And when he enrolled his daughter Amy in a public school near the White House, he did wonders in building up the image of a president who was close to the people.

His regional meetings were masterpieces of populism and he could even radiate folksiness on television.

An important factor has left American political life—the personal presidential campaign. It is difficult to picture any president ever again campaigning from the rear platform of a train, walking through huge street crowds gathered under tall buildings, shaking hands at outdoor rallies. The assassination of Robert Kennedy made it clear that such activities involve unacceptable risks even when the candidate is a challenger and not currently holding the office.

The personal campaign is not to be despised, despite its carnival air and the mindless character of the slogans and political speeches. As an educational device, it left something to be desired—but the American people did learn something from it. It gave voters an opportunity to observe a man under conditions of stress and excitement where his reactions and comments were unguarded. Some of the judgments made under those circumstances were exceptionally shrewd. No one can continue to play a role for week after week of grueling travel. Sooner or later psychological defenses will slip and the genuine character will emerge.

Even more important, it represented a form of communion between a leader and his people, a communion that was a two-way street. Voters who could see a man in person, perhaps even, with a little luck, get to touch him, somehow felt that they shared in the processes that governed them. Candidates, on the other hand, received a sense of drawing strength from the great mass.

Presidents and candidates for the presidency will, of course, continue to campaign, and science and technology have placed in their hands an instrument that solves the problem of security—television. Here is a device that can be perfectly controlled. It can be set up in a bombproof room, it requires so few people in the president's immediate vicinity that everyone can be checked and cross-checked to the complete satisfaction of the most cautious security officer, and it can enable a president to reach an audience running into nine figures.

From every standpoint it seems ideal. The lighting can be controlled to present the candidate in the most flattering manner; camera angles can be dictated to show what he considers most photogenic; TelePrompTers can unroll his script in the most readable form; and no other medium can bring a message to so many people at such a low cost per unit.

Of course, there are problems. Some presidents are not well adapted to television. Richard Nixon, in my judgment, actually lost people with all the money that he spent on TV. And Gerald Ford succeeded only in looking clumsy. Furthermore, every political appearance preempts some other program and many Americans become irritated when they lose their weekly *Miami Vice*. Nevertheless, these are questions of scheduling and technique. What is more important is that television snaps another link in the two-way communication that should exist between the president and the American people. Television is a one-way street.

This medium which replaces the face-to-face campaign is sufficiently peculiar to deserve a closer look. Television is at one and the same time the most personal and the most impersonal method of communication that has ever been contrived. It can bring a man into the living room, warm and vibrant, as a living presence. One hour later the same man can be watching himself on a replay with the detachment of a critic reviewing a theatrical performance. He can even write notes (and frequently does) directing himself on fine points that will improve his performance the next time around.

Few of us can literally stand outside ourselves and criticize our own performance without suffering some confusion in our identity. Unlike the old-time newsreel, which was shown under technical conditions that never permitted the viewer to forget that it was a mechanical device, television creates an illusion of immediate reality even though nothing is happening except the unreeling of magnetized tape through a series of spools. Even the screen on which the pictures are flashed is encased in a cabinet designed to blend into the surroundings.

A man (not every man) viewing his own performance as it actually happened can easily slide into a feeling of divinity, convinced that he possesses godlike powers to change his identity—to become a Winston Churchill or a Franklin Roosevelt or an Abraham Lincoln, if only he can find the right speech writers, voice coaches, and makeup artists. The feeling comes most easily to a man of strong ego living under circumstances that indulge all his personal desires. Most presidents are in that category.

To the actor, of course, this is not a problem, as his whole life consciously centers on the presentation of personalities other than his own. But a political leader, in order to carry out his functions, must have a number of aims of which making a presentation is only one, however important. In the age of television there is a strong temptation to subordinate all other priorities to the performance in a theatrical sense.

The preoccupation of presidents with television has increased as the years have gone by. Eisenhower brought Robert Montgomery into the White House as a coach and a "consultant." Kennedy made the transition to the live, televised press conference. Johnson installed a television studio in the White House and when he traveled he always took along his own TelePrompTers and crew. Nixon's aides chattered almost incessantly about the presidential "image," as built on TV with painstaking care.

The two presidents who have made the most effective use of television in my judgment have been Jimmy Carter and Ronald Reagan. Carter had an instinctive—if not conscious—recognition of the power of TV to communicate through symbols and its poor performance in communicating through words. His most effective presentation was his speech on energy conservation. He made it in the White House library before a fireplace, complete with burning logs, and he wore a sweater. I questioned dozens of people the following day and none of them remembered what he had said. But because of the fireplace and the sweater, all of them had "received the message." He was telling the American people that the days of cheap, convenient energy were over and they would have to learn to generate more of their own heat. As for Reagan, he is an absolute master at the production of easy smiles and hand waves that reassure everyone who sees them that God's in his heaven and all's right with the world.

The experiences of the presidents parallel the spread of television as the principal medium of communication in the United States—a potent force that cannot be ignored. But a great deal of the obsessive discussion in the White House goes far beyond the actual impact of electronics on the public. A large share arises out of the preemptive nature of the medium itself, the tendency of TV to set both the location and the timetable for an important event.

The cameras for most TV are clumsy. They take time to set up and even more time to check out. They raise questions of lighting, makeup, voice levels, background scenery. Above all, air time is precious and must be divided into fractions of minutes. All this means that it is usually easier to bring the story to the medium than the medium to the story.

Perhaps the epitome of this situation is the successful effort of the Johnson administration to persuade Congress to accept the State of the Union message in the evening rather than at the traditional noon session. This put the event in prime viewing time, although it is doubtful that it actually secured a larger audience, since the hour eliminated coverage on the major news shows between 6 and 7 P.M. Whether good or bad from a public-relations standpoint, however, it demonstrated the capacity of television to override the established habits of two major branches of the government.

The most graphic illustration of the effects of TV on our government is the White House press conference. When televised, this has become as spontaneous as a Javanese temple dance but without the grace that makes the latter so deeply moving. The realities are at their starkest when the conference is held in the East Wing, where facilities are generally lacking and must be improvised.

The reporters—in this instance supporting players rather than information seekers—are brought in early to pick their way to seats through the maze of cords and cables that litter the floor. Their roles are perfectly well understood. They are batting-practice pitchers, present to serve the ball up over the plate where the hitter can take a healthy swing. It is accepted practice that the first two questions will be allotted to the wire-services, and that the traditional "Thank you, Mr. President" will be uttered by the senior wire-service correspondent.

The show—and that is what it is—must start on time. The president enters the room on a cue from the chairman of the television and radio pool (a post that rotates with regularity) designed to put him on camera at the hour or the half hour. He mounts the dais, asks the correspondents to be seated, and proceeds with his announcements. He then opens himself to questions, with due obeisance, of course, to the wire-service understandings.

The trappings are impressive although not very aesthetic. On either side of the president (but out of the lens angles) are signal corps men with "shotgun" microphones, which they point at each correspondent who is recognized. Overhead is a rack designed to give him precisely the lighting he wants. The microphone into which he speaks is fed into a "mult"—a device that permits all the networks to pick up his voice without mounting extra microphones on the podium—which is also controlled by the signal corps.

There are rarely more than twenty questions, usually one to a correspondent. They are not controlled—this was tried with disastrous results on one or two occasions—because controls are unnecessary. The president completely dominates the scene. The lead questions are easily predictable. Follow-up questions—the kind that narrow down generalizations or pinpoint evasions—are nearly impossible in a situation where two-hundred to four-hundred correspondents are clamoring for recognition and where time is limited. Any president who has done his homework will emerge unscathed, with a generality for the "tough" questions and a rebuff for the "impertinent" ones. It is a breeze.

For Kennedy, who enjoyed the whole process hugely, it was a plus performance from which he emerged points ahead every time. This was to be expected. Interestingly enough, however, Johnson, who dreaded the televised news conference, also ended each session with a distinct improvement in his "public image." The cards are so stacked in favor of the White House that it does not take professional skill to win.

Televised press conferences, with rare exceptions, are cut off ruthlessly after twenty-eight minutes—a few less, if possible. The networks lose enough money devoting a half hour to a "public service" program. It would be mean to take them over that half hour where they would not only lose money but would be faced with the problem of improvising some kind of a presentation once a scheduled show had been ruined by an unexpected presidential preemption of a crucial segment of time.

Occasionally an offbeat question pops up, usually from a correspondent for a small newspaper. The president might receive an unexpected query about his views on the ultimate nature of life, his attitude toward television evangelism, or his reaction to proposals to make the turkey the national bird. Rarely does the question bear on important issues that are troubling a president. If he is witty, he can pick up some mileage with a quick response. If he is not, he can be noncommittal and no one will be hurt.

The obvious questions that arises is the point of the whole exercise. It does give the people an opportunity to hear their president discuss basic issues of the day, but the discussion would vary little if he instead appeared and read a series of statements without the presence of reporters as "props." This is all the performance can possibly amount to so long as time is limited and so many correspondents are seeking recognition.

Democracy, of course, requires rituals as much as any other form of government, and the televised news conference serves this purpose. It is at least equal—and in some respects superior—to the parliamentary question, which must be submitted in advance and which cannot take as many forms. But this is not the issue at stake. The salient point is that in a process that purports to be the supreme form of communication between a president and his people, the presentation has become the dominant factor. Performance, in a theatrical sense, rides roughshod over content. For all the public learns about a chief executive's thinking, the reporters might as well sit in the front lobby and dutifully file the press releases handed out by the press office.

None of this is to imply that we live in an age of political salesmen in contrast to a remote past in which our leaders were "statesmen." Throughout history, every politician has resorted to every device available to "sell" himself to his constituency. The difference now is that the politician has nothing to pull him down to earth except the Nielsen ratings, and those are always good where a president is concerned. The whole process is a performance, with a star who is also the producer and director and who is not going to let himself be upstaged. He can "project" his image with no more fear of face-to-face hostile reaction than the Queen of England when she makes a speech from the throne.

But no one in the modern world expects a queen or a king to actually run a government. There is almost universal agreement that a throne is an excellent platform from which to reign but an impossible platform from which to rule. It is far too comfortable, far too insulated from the harsh realities, to harden anyone against the exigencies of statecraft.

What has happened is that a device universally hailed as a boon to communication has become merely a means of one person talking to millions. It is a means by which a man can conduct a monologue *in* public and convince himself that he is conducting a dialogue *with* the public. Nothing can be more damaging to the psyche of an individual, and whatever damages a president damages the nation.

It may well be that every aspect of the presidency damages the psyche of the man who holds the office. It was conceived as an eminence—an area of unlimited authority, although within a limited sphere. As the power of the United States has increased, so has the responsibility of the president and so has his isolation. One does not deal in quite the same way with a man who can hurl the atomic bomb as one does with a man who can command only a couple of frigates or two or three regiments.

It is futile to study the problem of security and the

problem of public communication in the hope that forms can be found that will meet the first requirement and not cancel out the second. The simple rule of thumb is that the degree of security increases with the degree of isolation from the public and the degree of communication increases with the degree of public contact. Security and communication are mutually exclusive and the problem is not resolved by electronics. The latter merely adds to the confusion.

It is possible, of course, to conceive of forms of government in which neither would be a problem. A prime minister is not as vulnerable to assassination as a president and he owes his position to a parliamentary body that he must face frequently and whose members must in turn communicate through their parties with the electorate. But there is a vast gap between conception and accomplishment. Ours is not a parliamentary form of government and there is no reason to believe it will become one.

All that can be said with validity is that forces arising in the second half of the twentieth century have acted to increase the gap between the president and the people. The degree of presidential responsiveness has been diminished, and one more degree of darkness has been added to the shadows that are creeping over the American presidency as we have known it.

Chapter X

The End of an Era

IN TERMS OF public awareness, the monarchical presidency reached its climax in the administrations of Lyndon Johnson and Richard Nixon. They were miles apart in temperament, background, style, and political outlook. But they shared certain commonalities. Both were incredibly ambitious, incredibly energetic, incredibly daring, and incredibly tenacious. Furthermore, both at time exhibited symptoms of an inferiority complex and both were convinced that a snobbish eastern elite was looking down at them through symbolic monocles. What held them together most firmly, however, was a view of the American chief executive as the absolute center and focal point of life. They were in the power tradition established by Woodrow Wilson and Franklin Roosevelt. In point of fact, Nixon regarded Wilson as his role model and Johnson sought to emulate Roosevelt.

There were Wagnerian overtones to the departure of the two men from office. Johnson left to the tune of derisive sneers from a whole generation of college students turned off by Vietnam. During the closing days of his tenure, he became a veritable recluse in the White House, which was surrounded by half-naked youths chanting, "Hey, Hey, LBJ! How many kids have you killed today?" The man who once told me that he wanted to go down in history as "the education president" had become a pariah to those whose good opinion he valued the most. Nixon departed with dark clouds of scandal swirling around his head and forces of impeachment building up that almost certainly would have been successful had he not resigned. He had constructed his political career on the prosecution of Communists in the government and it ended with the prosecution of his followers for chicanery in the office of the presidency.

The debacle of the two administrators was sufficiently big to guarantee their places in history for dramatic quality alone. But there was more at stake than drama. Put together, Johnson and Nixon closed out an era. They left the nation with a sense of distrust for the office itself rather than just for the men who occupied it. The fact that Watergate—the source of the Nixon scandal—had followed so quickly on the heels of Vietnam struck many people as more than a coincidence. The question on everyone's mind was whether the presidency had become a rogue elephant out of control. Perhaps very few Americans stated the idea in such language. But it was notable that the next two presidents for whom they voted were men with no Washington stamp on them whatsoever. Furthermore, Congress was emboldened to take the step of putting some limits on the power of the president to send soldiers overseas without a declaration of war.

The War Powers Act, which was aimed directly at preventing a recurrence of the Korean and Vietnamese wars, has never received the analytical attention it deserves. Commentators have been so absorbed in pointing to its inadequacies that they have failed to realize the tremendous shift in public thinking that was signaled by its passage. Since the spring of 1939, no president had lost a battle with Congress over a foreign policy issue in which he truly believed. Even Harry Truman, who was denied virtually everything he requested in the domestic field, was able to secure approval of such ground-breaking international measures as the Marshall Plan, Point IV, and the Greek-Turkish Doctrine. Presidents might be resisted on the amounts of money involved and there were treaties such as the Genocide Convention or the Human Rights Covenant that languished in the Senate committee pigeonholes. But enough money was always appropriated to carry out the programs and the treaties never really had a top priority. It was taken for granted that foreign policy was a presidential prerogative and challenges to him in this area were less than "do or die" in intensity.

The congressional decision to put some limits on the presidential right to use American troops meant that something had snapped. The mystical trust in the chief executive had begun to fade in Korea and had virtually vanished in Vietnam. The institutionalization of the distrust in a specific piece of law meant that the office would never again be the same. The occupant of the White House would still be the prime mover in the foreign field. But for all future time he would have a congressional presence looking over his shoulder in the chambers of the National Security Council. Even Ronald Reagan, whose public popularity is phenomenal, finds that his foreign policy victories with Congress are narrow and invariably accompanied by conditions that most of his predecessors back to FDR would have been able to beat off.

In retrospect, it seems incredible that men of the political experience of Johnson and Nixon should have brought the presidency to such a pass. There were very early signs that Vietnam was a loser. And the cause of Watergate was incessant fretting over an election that Nixon could not have lost had the Democratic National Committee been awarded an exclusive franchise to count the ballots. There were points at which LBJ could have disengaged American troops from fighting in Southeast Asia without the disengagement resulting in a loss of honor. The burglary of the Democratic National Committee headquarters in Watergate was a demonstration of idiocy that still leaves Washington gasping in disbelief. What was there to find other than proof that the Democrats were broke—a condition that Larry O'Brien, the chairman, was proclaiming from the rooftops every day? The facts are that the two men were victims of the presidency itself—two men whom the White House had robbed of their normal perspectives of the world.

How we got into Vietnam and what the Republicans expected to find in Watergate are still mysteries to me. But I had a ringside seat on the forces that kept LBJ in a losing war. And I have seen enough of life in the White House to be able to make a fairly reasonable estimate on what plunged Nixon into such a foolish enterprise. It is worth following up on the two points in order to obtain some insight into the factors that brought down the two presidents as well as the presidency itself.

The most important consideration is the tendency of the federal bureaucracy at the very top levels (there may be sabotage below the top) to bend its efforts toward carrying out presidential policies. The assumption is that the goals have been settled and nothing remains other than a search for ways and means. Obviously, such a search *is* necessary, and obviously a government that spends all its time arguing policy will be ineffective. As long as the original decision is correct, there is nothing wrong with the process. But it becomes deadly when the original policy decision is *wrong*. Then all the steps taken to carry it out multiply the evil. The search for ways and means becomes a reinforcing device for the basic policy. And when the mistakes begin to mount, the advice to the president may merely set his mind in concrete. The few who have the temerity to counsel reevaluation find their voices drowned.

It is essential to be clear on this point and not go off on tangents of imaginary plots to lie to the president. I do not rule out mendacity altogether because it figures in human affairs. But I doubt that it is prevalent. What causes the trouble is the reception given to all of the events and facts coming into Washington that bear on a crucial foreign policy, to which a heavy commitment has been made. They are *not* studied in terms of whether they indicate success or failure of a basic decision. Instead, they are examined to determine whether a specific tactic has worked. When it has not worked, the tactic rather than the policy is blamed. When the basic commitment involves blood, there is an even greater danger. The policy may cease to be an intellectual guide to action which can be discussed in rational terms. Instead, it may become a crusade that must be pursued to the bitter end so soldiers who have lost their lives will not have died in vain. At that point, every setback becomes a spur to redoubled action rather than a warning to pull back and take another look.

I have no doubt whatsoever that this was the operative mechanism that pushed us so deeply into Vietnam. It became something of a struggle to vindicate the sacrifice of the Americans who had lost their lives fighting the Viet Cong. What began with a few GIs sent in as instructors soared to thousands as men were killed. The numbers went well past a mere presence, to over half a million. In response, the agencies of government searched frantically for new tactics to make the policy work. Strategic hamlets, pacification, defoliation, aerial bombing north of the line followed one another in bewildering succession. Each proposal presented to him convinced Johnson even more strongly that "the best minds" at his disposal approved of what was being done. About the only person who confronted him directly was Undersecretary of State George Ball, who thought the whole operation was futile. But his advice was so obviously his own rather than that of the institution he served that LBJ disregarded it totally. Presidents all develop a remarkable capacity to sleep with their eyes wide open when something is being said they do not want to hear. At lower levels in the agencies were people such as Townsend Hoopes who were waging a vigorous battle against what was being done. But their thoughts did not even penetrate the White House.

The key to the situation lies in the phrase "institutional advice." I suspect that all presidents develop a superstitious regard for advice that comes from the top agencies in national security. The presidency is a lonely job in which the burden of making ultimate decisions can be a positive torment. It is reassuring that there are agencies staffed by some of the finest minds—or at least by men and women who have been certified as having the finest minds—who can give comforting reassurance and support. In the case of Lyndon Johnson this reliance on top diplomatic and defense leaders at times became obsessive. He was not a reflective man who could see the roles played by different elements in the decision process. It would never have occurred to him that institutions act institutionally, which means that they cannot make the fundamental decisions for which we look to the president. Even further from his mind was the realization that tactical moves are governed by basic assumptions and the basic assumption of the governmental agencies is that they are there to carry out the will of the chief executive.

In a conversation with him, I once suggested that he call in the National Security Council members to a session of extraordinary secrecy and inform them that he had decided to pull out of Vietnam within two months. His charge to them would be to work out the best methods of doing it in order to maintain United States prestige, leave our defense intact, and salvage whatever we could of the South Vietnamese leaders who would be placed in jeopardy by the action. I did not make any great point of the suggestion; it was an informal occasion and I was just casting about for some means of getting different perspectives on the situation. At best, I was half serious. His reaction, however, was extraordinary. He looked at me as though I had committed blasphemy and told me in forceful terms that I was not to repeat such thoughts to anyone. This may well have been one of the major episodes that put an end to a relationship that once had been close. I did not follow up because at that point I had not developed full confidence in my thinking on the relationship of the president to the bureaucracy. In later years, when that period of my life came into better perspective, I regretted that I had not made an effort to persuade him to try out the proposal. I find it fascinating to speculate on what kind of advice he would have received.

It is worthwhile to trace—as far as they can be traced—the events that eventually led to his change of mind. Primarily, they center around Clark Clifford, a Washington lawyer who was brought to prominence under Truman and became a mover and a shaker under presidents of both parties for the two decades that followed. Johnson made him Secretary of Defense after Robert McNamara, who had developed qualms about the war in Vietnam, resigned the post.

Clifford has one of the shrewdest and deepest minds that ever existed in Washington. It was not immediately apparent, as he dressed, talked, acted, and looked like a family retainer lawyer from the pages of an Agatha Christie novel. Like his frame, his sentences were lean and revealed only that which he had decided to reveal. When he spoke, one became aware of extraordinary powers of concentration, and the vision of a mere actor reading lines resolved into a realization that he was formidable. I suspect that Cardinal Richelieu and Prince Kropotkin were very much like that. They too had mastered the arts of manipulating a monarch. In addition, they too had original thoughts.

For openers, Clifford asked the top strategic thinkers of the Pentagon what would be necessary to secure peace in Vietnam. The answer was military victory. The next question was what resources would have to be committed to secure victory. The answer was to invade North Vietnam with a force that went far beyond current military levels. Obviously, such commitments were unacceptable in a nation whose young people were on the verge of revolt against Selective Service machinery even when it was operating with comparatively low numbers. Thus there could be only one answer: Get out!

The questions that brought about the answer had not been asked previously because the administration's assumptions were not based on total victory. The concept had been one of punishing the North Vietnamese until they were ready to "make a deal" that would be advantageous to South Vietnam. Clifford was one of the few who grasped the fact that no amount of "punishment" would be sufficient, short of all-out war toward a "victory" that would risk bringing Communist China into the conflict and touching off not only World War III but perhaps World War final. Even more important, Clifford was the only person who had grasped the fact *and* who had the skill and the position to do something about it.

The craftsmanship of his operation had to be seen at close quarters to be credited and very little of it could be seen at close quarters. He may not have graduated from West Point but he understood fully the military concept of screening a flanking movement. I first realized that something unusual was going on at a Cabinet meeting where he had been assigned the role of briefing everyone on the war. He began by ostentatiously removing his wristwatch and propping it against some papers before him on the Cabinet table. "I have been assigned seven minutes to brief the Cabinet and I want to be certain that I do not exceed the allotted time," he said, in a voice so pompous I suspected something was up. I have a streak of perversity which impels me to time people who say things like that. I felt it was justified when, at the end of seventeen minutes, he picked up his watch and announced that he had reached the end of his seven minutes. There was something else about his remarks that did not jibe with his description of them. Somehow, they were loose jointed—not quite falling into line.

There were at least two more meetings before I realized what was happening. He was presenting the weakest possible case for staying in Vietnam, but presenting it in such a manner that he could not be accused of opposing the general policy. Furthermore, he spoke in soothing tones that sent everyone into a half-doze where they absorbed his words on a virtually subliminal basis. Over a period of time, they would come to recognize the holes in the rationale and would almost certainly turn against the war—and think it was their own idea. I do not know how he worked on the president directly when they were alone, but there is little doubt in my mind that he turned LBJ around in such a way that LBJ decided it was his own idea. Before the year was out, the president was moving every possible lever to bring the North Vietnamese to the bargaining table in Paris. I believe that one of the major factors in Johnson's decision not to run for reelection in 1968 was his realization that he could not succeed in securing a conference as long as the North Vietnamese could look on his peace overtures as an election ploy to cater to war disaffected forces in the United States.

After he left the White House, Johnson indignantly denied that Clifford had anything to do with his conversion. The denial was probably sincere. He had been worked on by a master of the fine art of convincing a monarch that he had come to a decision all by himself.

The phrase "all by himself" is the key to the White House. All of the characteristics that make the office so different from any other in our experience flow from the simple fact that the president is without peers, let alone superiors. There is no one who can tell him authoritatively that he had done right or has done wrong. Down the road, the voters will pass judgment on the quality of his performance. Outside the walls of the establishment, there is a constant drumfire of critics who, after the famous initial honeymoon, will scream that he is leading the nation down the road to perdition. But the verdict of the voters comes far too late to act as a standard against which conduct can be measured and the critics can be dismissed as armchair observers who have axes to grind and who came to their conclusions without the responsibility of having to take the consequences for their outcome.

There is a comfort in the presence of peers and superiors whose judgment on what we do is authoritative. They give us some stable platforms upon which to stand as we plot our travel through life. We may often go against their judgment but we do so in the full consciousness that we are stepping outside the normal means of doing business. We may defy the gods but at least we know the consequences of defiance and who the gods are. It is when we must act without knowing the normal standards of conduct and with no one to judge the action other than ourselves that our minds begin to totter. To have no standard other than our own introspection is to play God, something human beings do very poorly.

Everyone who has decision authority runs into this phenomenon to some degree. But there is no position in the United States in which the isolation from equals is so complete as in the presidency. To be the absolute superior in status to everyone else encountered throughout the day is an effective form of isolation, even if it is not accompanied by legal powers of physical control over other people. In many respects, it is an even more effective form of isolation than physical confinement. The prisoner doing a spell in solitary *knows* that he is cut off from other human beings. The president, however, is surrounded by large, adoring groups that give him the illusion of human contact when all they really do is act as an echo chamber for his thoughts. This is the cause of the many aspects of presidential behavior that are so strikingly similar to the conduct of kings and czars during the great days of monarchy.

Even an absolute despot must have someone around who can say some salty, impudent things to spice immeasurably dull conversations. In the palaces of those who ruled by divine right, there was usually a court jester, a person who was known to be somewhat off his rocker. He had the privilege of delivering tart remarks for which anyone else would have found himself scheduled for an early morning appointment with the headsman. It was safe because who would pay any attention to the thoughts of a fool? I invite anyone to look back on the administrations that are within his or her memory and look at the "court jester." I do not intend to name any of them but people with some knowledge of the White House will catch my point immediately. In every case it was a personal attendant—almost at the level of a valet—who was not going to be taken seriously as an adviser. He could say what others could not because it was regarded as a mere diversion from the serious business of government.

Another parallel to monarchical courts is the phenomenon of the palace favorite, the person who suddenly becomes the top dog whatever his title might be. This is less a function of the favorite's ability to solve problems than his ability to assure the chief executive that he is authoritative. In a monarchy, the road to success is to provide the monarch with a psychological feeling of stability. The person who succeeds in filling this role may be ill adapted to the tasks that are assigned to him. But when he becomes known as the president's favorite, it doesn't matter. He has all the powers of the presidency at his disposition for as long as the president cares to let him have them. Usually the hand is overplayed somewhere along the line, which accounts for the fact that most administrations produce three or four favorites at different times during its course.

In terms of Watergate, what is relevant is the feeling of paranoia that every president develops at some point. The position is so unstructured that the chief executive can never be absolutely certain that what is being said or done in the outside world is innocent of any desire to frustrate his intentions. The office is at such a lonely eminence that no standard rules of the political game govern the approaches to it. Johnson told fascinating stories about the tactics he had used, while still a member of the House, to extract favors from FDR. He made a practice of driving Roosevelt's secretary, Grace Tully, to the White House every morning. This gave him an opportunity to drop words in her ear, give her memoranda knowing she would pass them on to the "boss," and learn personal characteristics that he could exploit at a later date. He once filed away in his memory the knowledge that Roosevelt was passionately interested in the techniques of dam construction. A few months later, he wangled his way into the White House with a series of huge photographs of dams that had been supplied to him by an architectural firm in his home district. Roosevelt became so absorbed in comparing the pictures that he absentmindedly okayed a rural electrification project that Johnson wanted but that had been held up by the Rural Electrification Administration for a couple of years.

Both Johnson and Nixon were well aware of the intrigue that swirls constantly around the White House. They were also familiar with the kind of partisan warfare that is played constantly in Washington by leaking stories to the press. Consequently, they both sought a "leak-proof" White House and staffs that would play the games solely under presidential direction. They were also convinced that outside the White House wall were enemies engaged in organized conspiracies to bring them down. LBJ thought that most of those plots centered around Bobby Kennedy. Nixon thought of them as emanating from "liberal" Democrats. There is no doubt in my mind that Bobby Kennedy did *not* like LBJ and lost no opportunity to cut at him. Neither is there any doubt in my mind that Democrats carried normal, partisan warfare beyond the bounds of reason where Nixon was concerned. But the concept of deep, dark plots was utterly ridiculous. Had the men been living among peers, their fears would have encountered a good-humored set of rejoinders that would at least have softened them.

Nobody to whom he listens really argues with a president about such things. The purpose of the White House staff is supportive, not argumentative. Consequently, presidential anxieties not only lack counterbalancing counsel, they meet positive reinforcement. As the anxieties grow, so does the reinforcement role of the staff. In very little time the whole establishment takes on the air of a beleaguered fortress. In the closing days of my own service, I reached a point where I dreaded going to the White House mess to eat lunch. The gloom engendered by the siege mentality was so thick that food could not be enjoyed.

Even though I had no inside seat in the Nixon White House, it is easy to see how growing paranoia led to Watergate. The actions taken were those of desperate men who believed that their political lives were at stake. Even more important, they shared the illusion of all politicians that the welfare of the nation required their continued presence in office. I often wonder how many of the people who condemned the Watergate conspirators would have acted had they been part of the White House staff at the time.

This does not mean that the Watergate scandals are common in American political life. I believe I am reasonably familiar with both the written and the unwritten political history of recent years and I doubt whether any White House of the past ever engaged in such activity. It was a violation of common understandings that have governed politicians throughout our history. If anything, it demonstrated that the inhabitant of the executive mansion does not play by the same rules that govern other politicians.

The final crash was traumatic. Even though history may deal more kindly with Richard Nixon than did his contemporaries (his opening to China, for example, was historic), the presidency had reached a point where there had to be a sudden halt and an opportunity for reassessment. The Roosevelt era had come to a close and there were problems that could not be solved on the spot. Nixon's last official act was to clear the way for a caretaker—a spare, somewhat awkward man whose outstanding characteristic was a blunt honesty. His greatest virtue, perhaps, was that in the era of giant monarchical presidents, Gerald Ford would never have been considered as a candidate. The American people were given a chief executive whose character was totally out of step with the immediate, very unhappy past.

Chapter XI

The Caretaker Presidents

THE CRASH THAT brought an end to the Roosevelt era was followed by a spell of caretaker presidents. The suspicions of the White House engendered by both Vietnam and Watergate were too strong to give scope to another activist chief executive. For the first, this was not particularly a problem. Gerald R. Ford was not, by temperament, an innovator or a "busy-busy" doer. Furthermore, the task before him when he took over from Nixon did not call for frenetic activism. His job was to convince the American people that the White House had been cleansed from a noisome presence and once again was in the hands of people who could be trusted to be honest even if not always right. For this, he was superbly equipped—a rugged, straightforward man of transparent honesty who positively radiated the simple virtues of small-town America. At a time when citizens wanted no city slickers, he could not have been better cast for the role by Paramount Studios.

For the second successor to Nixon, however, the period must have been one of excruciating agony. Jimmy Carter was an "activist" in every sense of the word—a born again Baptist with a sense of mission and an engineer's ingrained determination to concentrate all of his faculties on a project until it was completed. His major asset with the public was probably his roots in rural

America and his nonidentification with the Washington scene. But his major asset in life had been self-discipline and an unrelenting search for achievement. In another period of history he might well have entered the exclusive club of "great presidents," the movers and shakers who stand as milestones in American history. He was certainly not afraid of new ideas, he was certainly in step with the spirit of technology that dominates our nation, and he was certainly a man who could make decisions and stand by them. Unfortunately for him, American society had no intention of being moved or shaken about anything. There was no nationwide consensus as to a course that should be followed.

The American system is not one that depends on "strong" or fails with "weak" people in office. What it really does is produce strong men when it is in array and weak men when it is in disarray. The strong presidents— Washington, Jackson, Lincoln, Wilson, and the Roosevelts—have appeared when there was a consensus, or at least enough of one to permit action. When the system is in transition—when the older forms of politics are dying and the newer forms have yet to attain strength—so-called weak men are thrown up to the top. At no time can it ever be said with certainty that the United States has found the "best" man for the job. But it usually finds the "right" man, someone who reflects the times. On those occasions when the president is not in the mainstream, he suffers.

I think of Carter as one who suffered. Virtually nothing of any moment was done during his administration and to the extent that he will be remembered in popular legend it is as the born again president who "lusted in his heart after women" and who beat off an attack from a killer rabbit charging his canoe. The most historic event of his four years in office was his failure to find a means of releasing the hostages held in the American embassy by the Iranian government. The fact that the Iranians waited until the last day of his term to let their captives go was a crowning indignity.

The experiences of both Ford and Carter are not new in American history. There have been many periods in which the presidency was reduced to a state of virtual helplessness only to emerge after a period of time under the control of a man of considerable strength. This has led to numerous "cyclical" theories of American politics—the concept that innovators must be followed by periods of consolidation and then by further periods of innovation. I have no argument with these theories, nor do I propose to indulge in an essay on semantics. I merely advance the thought that it is more useful, in terms of understanding what is happening to us now, to think of the process as a political system that *must* respond to changes in the social structure. This point is best made by examining the most dramatic slump in presidential prestige in our history, the period that preceded the Civil War.

It is generally agreed that the years from 1848 to 1860 represented a low point in the saga of the presidency. The three men who occupied the office during that period can be named only by academic specialists in the office or experts at trivia quiz games. So my readers will not be tantalized, they were Millard Fillmore, Franklin Pierce, and James Buchanan. Perhaps the best measure of their standing in the presidential pantheon is that the readiest source of information concerning their lives is a book entitled *The Presidents, Tid Bits and Trivia*. Fillmore was the first sitting president to be denied renomination by his own party; Pierce was opposed to slavery but most of his friends were slaveholders; Buchanan thought that the South had no right to secede but that the North had no right to force it to remain in the Union.

These presidents reflected the general state of American politics at the time. The previous decade had seen a flourishing of some of America's greatest leaders. It had been the age of Webster, Clay, Calhoun, Hart, and Benton. These men all departed the scene at about the same time to be replaced by nonentities. Even more important was the status of our political parties. The Democrats split along North-South lines and the Whigs disappeared completely, to be replaced by political groups such as the Barn-Burners, the Conscience Whigs, and the Free-Soil Whigs. One of the more ominous developments was the rise of the Native American Party—the "Know Nothings" —who reveled in anti-Catholic bigotry directed against the Irish, who had suddenly swarmed into the eastern big cities because of the potato famine in their home country. Fillmore actually ran for president on the Know Nothing ticket after he was rejected for renomination by the Democrats.

It is customary to ascribe the confusion of the period to the issue of slavery. There is, however, another way of looking at it. It was not only a period of North-South divisiveness. It was also a period of deep social and economic transition that changed the whole face of American society. For the first time, the United States received a flood of non–Anglo Saxon immigrants—the potato-famine Irish and the Germans and Hungarians fleeing the unsuccessful revolutions that swept central Europe in 1848. And the industrialization of the country stepped up to a pace that was almost frantic. During the twelve years, seventeen thousand miles of railroad track were laid, the Spinning Jenny and Hargraves Mule came to the United States to lay a foundation for the textile industry, and the patent office went from a leisurely seven or eight patents a year to over a thousand. We were passing from an agricultural and trading society to a factory economy. We had the tools, we had the resources, and we had cheap labor knocking at the gates. The outcome was inevitable.

Against this background, the Civil War, usually thought
of as divisive, was in fact a unifying force. It did not heal
the breach between North and South, but it did set up
stable political systems that dominated the nation for
more than a century. In the South, the Democratic party
was established as a device to sustain segregation and
maintain white supremacy. In the North, the Union veterans formed the Grand Army of the Republic, which
became the backbone of the Republican party, which in
turn became an alliance between the Free Soil farmers
who had fought the war and the forces of industrialization. The Democratic party ranks were augmented by the
influx of immigrants from mainland Europe, but they
remained in the cities and did not play a major role on
the national scene until well into the twentieth century.

Even though the political structure was stable, the
nation remained in a state of transition during most of
the last part of the nineteenth century. The clash between agricultural and industrial interests became increasingly heated and the immigrants, at first docile in their
factory jobs, became restless and started to form organizations intended to give them greater economic bargaining power. What now appears idyllic—America at the
turn of the century—was actually a period of turmoil.
The presidents from Lincoln to Theodore Roosevelt were
almost as anonymous as those of the 1850's (Ulysses
Grant is remembered because of his military record and
Grover Cleveland because he was the only Democrat),
and political action on the national level revolved around
Congress—a center of boodlery whose major employment appears to have been the dispensation of juicy land
grants and other plums from the public domain. After
1875, the blacks no longer counted. They simply disappeared on the same plantations where they had been
held as chattel slaves. One could not detect a "before
and after" difference in their lives.

The early part of the twentieth century brought more stability and some truly strong presidents—Theodore Roosevelt, William Howard Taft, and Woodrow Wilson. They were followed by a group of presidents who made everyone's list of the ten worst (Warren Harding, Calvin Coolidge, Herbert Hoover) and then by Franklin Roosevelt, who was not only a strong president but the one who set the terms of the political dialogue. He established the conviction among Americans that the federal government has an obligation to intervene in the lives of its citizens in order to protect them from—or at least ease the impact of—economic adversity. With this as his guiding principle, he set up a coalition of agriculture, labor, immigrants, and intellectuals that made him invincible at the polls. There was no opposition to him other than diehard descendants of the Free Soil farmers and leading industrialists, who found themselves outflanked by FDR at every turn.

The depth of the Roosevelt revolution is difficult to comprehend for anyone who did not live before it. Prior to 1932, Americans did not expect the federal government to step into their lives and help them out. The populists had campaigned for federal policies that would provide cheap credit for farmers, and the era of literary muckraking had led to national statutes intended to protect consumers from contamination and adulteration of commodities. But the use of central authority to enhance the lives of individuals economically, to care for those who had fallen between the cracks in our society, and to abolish inequities was still regarded as heresy. If you needed political help, you went to see your precinct captain and that was that. It took an economic catastrophe to change the national attitude.

The presidents who followed FDR were not inconsiderable men. Of course, the innovations of the New Deal plus his role in World War II left behind a picture of a political giant who would make everyone else look lesser by comparison. But Truman, Eisenhower, Kennedy, Johnson, and Nixon are not going to disappear into the limbo that swallowed the chief executives of the last part of the nineteenth century. Watergate and Vietnam marked the close of the New Deal era. But in view of history, one cannot help but wonder whether those events merely exacerbated the forces that brought the era to a close. Is it possible that our society is once again undergoing deep economic and social changes that are rendering political leadership ineffective until they are completed? The answer in my mind is very clearly in the affirmative.

During the past two decades there have been developments that are staggering when viewed in historical perspective. We have had the black revolution, the women's lib movement, the emergence of the "gays" to the verge of respectability, and the rapid growth of a technological society that threatens to create large-scale masses of human beings who are superfluous to our economy. Less than one hundred years ago, many farm families were producing large numbers of children because they were economic assets as well as creatures to love. Today, we speak in grim terms of "triage" and abortion—while it still has strong opponents—has legal protection in order to hold down the population. Birth control is not only respectable but is regarded as a mark of social responsibility, and, above the ranks of the poor and the illiterate, it is taken for granted that families will be small.

Perhaps the heaviest impact of modern times is felt by the skilled manual workers. They are becoming a dying breed. The combination of the computer and automation have not only eliminated the need for human beings on the belt-line but have also enabled industry to produce commodities more cheaply. In the past, automation was usually accompanied by an increase in skilled workers among the service industries. Now the service industries themselves are becoming automated, as anyone can discover very quickly by patronizing self-service gasoline stations or extracting money from a "TYME" machine outside the local bank or inside the chain food market. As for the jobs themselves, the amount of muscular activity has been reduced to a point where people feel they must go out in the streets and run around aimlessly for an hour or so in order to make up for the loss of muscle tone that they once got from working. (Of course, they also jog to stimulate the economy in terms of larger sales of jogging suits, headbands, and portable radios to carry with them.)

The net effect of all this is to make people interchangeable in the work force. It takes no violent wrench of the psyche to go from a check-out clerk in a supermarket (where the cash register has become so automated that the ability to make change is no longer a prerequisite), to a bank teller, to a payroll accountant in a factory, to a librarian, to a travel agent, ad infinitum. All that is required is the punching of a different set of keys, and with some redesign, it would be possible to extend the list to virtually every occupation in our entire society. Huge plants are under construction that will employ only a handful of workers, and the announcement of a new plant is no longer a cause for a town's rejoicing over new jobs that will be created. Industrialization is past the point where it expands opportunities to job seekers; instead, it is closing them out and one cannot but wonder what will happen to markets when there are no longer huge reservoirs of income-earning workers to buy goods.

Our only concern in this book is whether these changes have an impact upon our political system. The answer is that they certainly do. Basic to American politics has always been the political broker—the expert at finding the necessary compromises that enable different groups to live together and make at least minimum progress.

This depends, however, on groups that have a strong feeling of identity and can be relied on to react as a unit to the political realities of their times. In the past, these groups were largely economic. They could be identified as farmers, blue-collar workers, white-collar workers, small business people, industrialists, and professionals. Each one of these groups, naturally, had subdivisions. A wheat farmer would react to political proposals in a far different manner than a cattle rancher. A coal miner would have a far different outlook than a garment worker. Doctors would not have the same set of priorities as accountants. But none of this changed the basic rules of political brokerage. It meant only that some solutions were more complicated than others.

The old economic groups can no longer be relied on to act as units. This is not just a function of automation. It is also a result of a more fluid society. Steel-mill workers who once lived in company houses in company towns now occupy suburban bungalows where they can drive to work. On Labor Day, they no longer go to Union Hall to hear speeches followed by a union picnic in a nearby park. Instead, they bundle up the family and head for the countryside or, if they are near enough, they take a motor trip to Disneyland. As for farmers, they do not need to rely on Sears Roebuck to sell them the necessities of life, and even in the most remote areas, they can get their entertainment from television. They no longer depend upon circuit-riding ministers with a Bible and a hymnal in their saddlebags.

For the politicians of the Roosevelt era, these changes were little short of traumatic. I had an opportunity to witness them up close in Hubert Humphrey's campaign for the presidency in 1968. Humphrey was the quintessential New Deal politician of the times—a combination of populist, labor backer, and protector of Jewish and black minorities (the women's movement had not be-

come a major force at that time and I have often wondered how he would have reacted to it). Basically, he
thought in terms of the moving issues of his youth—rural
electrification, union protection, oppressed minorities.
To him, these were still causes that made the pulse beat
and the feet march in quick time to combat the forces of
reaction. The result was a series of major disappoint-
ments. The rural electrification co-ops had become mere
service organizations that could not even turn out crowds
for his rallies. The only labor union that could fill a hall
for him was the postal workers, who had obvious reasons
for wanting to stand in well with a possible president.
Only the black and liberal Jewish organizations contrib-
uted the spirit and the drive that he associated with
campaigning.

It would be an error to conclude that Humphrey lost
the election because some of the major elements of his
coalition had lost their zest for political combat. He was
an attractive leader and might have won had he not been
Johnson's vice-president. He was forced to carry the
unpopularity of his predecessor, a kind of guilt by association. Nevertheless, it is significant that the groups that
did maintain their fighting edge were not basically economic. The common bonds that held blacks and Jews
together were ties of race, religion, and ethnicity just as
the bonds that later held together the members of the
women's and gay movements were ties of sexual identity.
Of course, there were economic aspects to both of the
latter groups, but they were spurs rather than instruments of unity.

The handling of social issues has never been the glory
of the American politician. The huge waves of immigra-
tion from Ireland and eastern and southern Europe during the last part of the nineteenth and the first part of the
twentieth centuries caused social problems. But it was
relatively easy to put them on the back burner. Growing

industry welcomed the immigrants because they provided a source of cheap labor and usually were taken over by political machines that kept them docile by a judicious dispensation of favors. On the national level, it was unnecessary to appeal for their votes, as those were obtainable only through deals with political bosses. Most of these were Democrats for the simple reason that the Republicans represented employers and there was an elite ambience to the GOP that did not attract ethnics.

Dealing with the ethnic groups was a far different problem from that of dealing with the social groups that dominate the thinking of contemporary society. The absorption of Europeans into the mainstream of America took time and toil. But it did not require a revolution. It merely meant hard work, learning the language, getting an education, and at times some subtle changes in name spelling. Life was hard; the obstacles were great. The outcome, however, was certain. The path out of the ethnic slum was clear: work. For blacks, women, and gays, the path was not at all clear and the outcome definitely not certain. The first two had been assigned social roles that made them inferior in the management of our society and the third was looked on as a group of loathsome criminals. The "liberation" of any of them was not going to be achieved by a display of the sturdy virtues inherent in the work ethic but required Americans to revise their long-held concepts of right and wrong.

The revolution was "accomplished"—at least to the extent of varying degress of protective legislation—through some of the most heated arguments of our time and, in the case of the blacks, a considerable amount of violence. The extent to which conditions have been improved for the three groups is arguable. Blacks still suffer the highest unemployment rates in our society; several studies have shown that women lag considerably behind men in terms of income; and the attitudes of society toward "gays" is still ambivalent as Anita Bryant demonstrated in some crusades to repeal protective city ordinances for them. Nevertheless, the official attitude of society has been changed on all counts. It is no longer respectable to keep a black out of your neighborhood because you "draw the color line," to deny a woman a job in a slaughterhouse because it is "desexing," or to refuse to rent a room to a homosexual or a Lesbian because you fear his or her moral influence on children.

Our political leaders have passed legislation banning discrimination against the three groups and that is about as far as they can go. Unfortunately, it is not as far as the problems go. It is easier to ban discrimination than it is to enforce that ban, and in any case, laws alone do not make up for the social inheritance that inevitably flows from more than three centuries of life in the lower depths, do not establish new social rules governing the relationships between men and women, and do not do away with the uneasy feeling that so many people have as to the moral influence of homosexuality. The issues of raw discrimination have been settled, but where do we go from here? There could be no poorer time to find a solution. All these issues impinge on us at a moment when we have run short of the resources that our government has used to solve social problems in the past—the financial strength of federalism.

Has these problems surfaced in the past, they would have been met by enormous social programs running into billions of dollars. There would have been special training programs for blacks beginning before kindergarten; industry would have been provided subsidies to absorb women into the work force without displacing men; even gays would probably have received some form of federal largesse. This was the dream of the "Great Society" that Lyndon Johnson managed to enact into law but not into reality. The legislation was passed and the structures of government were established, but there was not enough money. It was all going into a war in Vietnam that not only could not be won but that was going to produce no economic benefits that would make up for the cost. Since then, the role of the federal government in social engineering has been all downhill—slowly at first but now an accelerating descent that can bring the entire social welfare concept of government down to ground zero.

In retrospect, Johnson's "Great Society" programs may have had a negative impact on the willingness of Americans to trust such efforts. The passage of the bills through Congress gave a nationwide impression of a great crusade to abolish poverty and bring blacks to a status of par with whites in our society. There was little or no stress upon the fact that little muscle was going into the programs once they were enacted. The first to appreciate this fact were the blacks themselves, who begin to wonder whether they had been sold another bill of goods by "Whitey." This led to demonstrations and degrees of violence that led the whites to regard the blacks as ingrates who were repaying the efforts of white society to give them a break by tearing things to pieces. These were thoughts that definitely figured in the riots that hit our major cities in 1968.

At the time this is written, the prospect for social programs is so remote as to be unworthy of comment. Liberals and conservatives are vying with each other on cutting spending and restoring balance—or at least acceptable levels of deficit—to the federal budget. The only real arguments are over the targets for the major cuts. Liberals seek to gouge heavier chunks out of national defense spending; conservatives are trying to accelerate the slashes in social spending. Neither can produce a strong consensus, and this means that whatever happens will happen slowly and innovation will get short shrift. The public (if the polls can be believed) seems to

have lost its confidence in the ability of the federal government to resolve social problems anyway.

This is an age in which, outside of the field of foreign
affairs, presidents can be only caretakers. And even in
the international arena their prerogatives have been restricted. Congress has laid down some rules that can be
used to prevent another Vietnam and possibly even another Korea. I hasten to add that the fact they *can* be
used does not mean that they *will* be used. Nevertheless,
the mere fact that they exist is significant. Since Roosevelt got rid of the arms embargo, presidents have had a
virtually free hand once they raised problems beyond our
shores. Congressional restraints, even if they are ineffective, mark the dawn of a new day.

Chapter XII

Where Do We Go from Here?

IN THE LAST chapter, I carefully avoided a mention of Ronald Reagan. This is not because I consider him a departure from the line of caretaker presidents. If anything, he is the epitome of the caretaker—someone who knows how to keep the various groups of our society a bit off balance so they cannot combine to depose him and, at the same time, someone who knows how to create the illusion of action when not very much is actually going on. In my mind, he is strongly reminiscent of Louis Napoleon, who managed to stay on top in France for more than two decades because the really strong forces in the nation could not get together and select someone who would run things. Louis Napoleon could have stayed even longer had he not made the mistake of doing something—of getting into a war with Prussia. I hope Reagan draws the lesson.

What necessitates special consideration for Reagan is his political stability in an age of unstable politics. It has nothing to do with his programs. No poll has yet found enthusiastic acceptance of his economic concepts. Nor does it seem to me that his ascendancy represents a "turn to the right" on the part of the voters. Reagan may label himself a conservative and may espouse causes dear to the hearts of the far right wing such as antiabortion and school prayer constitutional amendments. But this is just enough to prevent the "true believers" from coming out against him openly, and the chances of anything happening on his constitutional amendments are virtually nil. The real high priests of fundamentalist politics cannot desert him, but they make little secret of their uneasiness as to his dedication to their cause. It does not matter. Reagan could win reelection today just as easily as he won it in 1984 and I doubt that his popularity will markedly decrease. I am not certain that the American people support him in the sense of backing his policies. But they are comfortable with him and that is what counts.

This is not the traditional course followed by presidents in an era of transition. Historically, they have tended to be men who happened to be standing in the right place at the right time and were pushed into office by crowds rushing up the street. Few of them had any real degree of popularity and those who did quickly lost it. They have come and gone with shifting social tides and nobody missed them when they left. Reagan is regarded with an affection that has not surfaced in the past.

When I look for parallels, the only ones I can find are in the realm of constitutional monarchy. Neither good times nor bad times seem to affect the esteem in which the British and Scandinavians hold their monarchs. They serve as unifying symbols and as such they are very useful. A member of the British Labour party can lift his glass to "Her Majesty, the Queen" with all the enthusiasm of Margaret Thatcher, and the royal families of the Nordic bloc are greeted as warmly by socialists as by captains of industry. It is much too early to come to any conclusion that we are on our way to an Americanized constitutional monarchy. But the satisfaction our people have with a chief executive who is not really changing things cannot be dismissed as mere coincidence. At the very least, it indicates that the true strength of the office lies in its symbolic role as the personification of the nation rather than in its managerial aspects.

What is bothersome about this is its failure to find a new wellspring for innovation in our society. Historically, the presidency has been the cutting edge for change. It is a role that cannot be filled by any of our other institutions. Congress, at its very best, can only resolve political differences and occasionally prod a president into action. The courts can bring about some social changes but only when they are confronted with legal cases that can be handled only by change. Only the man in the White House can lay down a consistent plan for change and marshal the forces that will bring it into effect.

Parliamentary democracies have solved the problem of instituting social change by giving political parties a role in the government itself and allowing the legislative body to select the prime minister, who manages the nation's affairs. There is no prospect of transition to a parliamentary government in the United States. The wrench to our system would be far too complicated. It would require the abolition of the federal system and the creation of totally new political parties. By the time we had mastered all of the new machinery, we would probably have disappeared as a nation.

What does seem worth a look, however, is the unusual degree of power Cabinet officers seem to enjoy in the Reagan administration. It is entirely impressionistic on my part, but I cannot avoid the feeling that the Secretary of State and the Secretary of Defense have a degree of autonomy that was not held by their predecessors. Both command a bureaucracy so huge that it could well be out of the control of the White House. I do not want to draw too strong a conclusion from this observation, but the transition of the British cabinet from being a creature of the king to being a creature of Parliament stemmed from a lazy monarch who did not like to attend cabinet meetings.

During my period in the White House, I made an interesting discovery: The bureaucracy has a life of its own and, without constant prodding, will set a course that bears no relationship whatsoever to the political imperatives of the president. An energetic chief executive who cares about what he is doing can force it to stay in line with his policies. But he must constantly ride herd on the responsible agencies—not just on the department secretary but on many of his subordinates. Lyndon Johnson exercised pinpoint control over every bomb that was dropped in Vietnam and probably knew the disposition of American forces better than did the Joint Chiefs of Staff. But the rest of the government ran itself once his absorption in Southeast Asia became total.

Sometimes an agency can resist a president to a point of virtual exhaustion. John Ehrlichman tells a fascinating story about Nixon's efforts to rid Washington of the Navy "tempos" on the mall. These were unsightly buildings that had been erected during *World War I* to house a munitions agency established under Woodrow Wilson. The war was over by the time they had been completed and the Navy moved in to use them "temporarily." More than fifty years later, they were still occupied despite the fact that they were excrescences on one of the loveliest vistas in Washington. The Navy had lined the ugly shells with luxurious offices in which assistant secretaries and admirals could be housed in an atmosphere that gave each one of them the feeling of monarchical splendor.

The helicopter flight to Andrews Air Force base that presidents take when they are going to travel finally did them in. Nixon could not help but notice the manner in which they ruined the landscape and he assigned Ehrlichman the task of getting them torn down. At that point, Ehrlichman was at the very top (shared with Haldeman) of the White House heap—a man known to speak with all the authority of the president. His word was as close to law as that of anyone in the executive branch of the government except the top man himself. Yet it took him nearly two years—with the Navy fighting every step of the way—to get rid of eyesores which had been put up as temporary buildings more than half a century earlier.

This, of course, is merely a straw in the wind. I do not want to read too much into it. Nevertheless, it is significant that on an issue so trivial, the bureaucracy can slow down the president. It demonstrates a potential for power resting on control of the agencies, agencies whose size and computerized methods of operation are so huge that their control is a full-time job. The president, even though he is not nearly as "busy" as the popular imagination pictures him, does not have that kind of time, because it does not exist. His only contact with the agencies as a whole lies in the monthly Cabinet meetings, which are purely cosmetic in character—"happenings" that are staged because Americans have accepted a myth that the Cabinet is supposed to do something. The real power of the Cabinet secretaries exists when they are back in their departments. But even then, it exists only to the extent that they have mastered the inner workings of a highly complex social organism whose individual units were in place long before they came to Washington and will remain in place long after they have left.

The intractability of some of the agencies is legendary. No former Secretary of Defense feels that he was *really* in charge. And most of the secretaries of health, education and welfare, before that department was split into two agencies, readily concede that they were never able to make any sense out of the sprawling monstrosity. They have, however, been under a rough form of control because they depend on Congress to supply their funds and on the president to dispense those funds. They can be called to account despite their many opportunities to obfuscate those to whom they are responsible.

At this point another possibility must be considered. It arises out of the Gramm-Rudman bill, which history may well record as one of the most significant events in the last half of the twentieth century as far as the operation of the government is concerned. This measure proposes to turn over the decisions about how much money would be spent to computers and faceless bureaucrats without political accountability. In view of the age-old axiom that the most important parliamentary power is the power of the purse, this bill is astounding. Nevertheless, it was enacted into law because the members of Congress admit that they cannot make the deep spending cuts that are absolutely essential. The budget is out of control.

It is possible that the Gramm-Rudman bill will be vitiated by the courts. Part of it has been knocked out already. But a congressional action need not result in an effective law in order to be significant. The mere fact that it is passed indicates both a mood and a trend. The mood is one of despair over the fiscal situation in which the nation finds itself. The trend is toward a search for impersonal means of correcting the staggering deficits so that no one need bear the onus of depriving Americans of federal assistance on which they have come to rely.

The temptation the Gramm-Rudman approach offers to Congress is obvious. The percentage of the federal budget that can be cut under *any* circumstances is not very large if one excludes defense spending. It is impossible to cut payments of the interest on the federal debt, one of the largest items. Veterans' pensions are an obligation of conscience as well as being statutory. The so-called entitlement programs, such as social security, cannot be cut without changing the law, and anyway it would lead to a revolution. No one disputes that much of the Defense Department budget is wasted. But no one is sure what part and few are willing to take the chance of a heavy slash.

Furthermore, a peculiar development of modern times makes it often more expensive to close something down than to keep it going at reduced levels. When I was in the White House, the issue was raised of the feasibility of shutting off the Houston Space Center. It was found that closing it would cost far more than slowing it down for a number of years in the hope that eventually it could be brought down to the zero level. This was because of the severance pay owed to the employees who could not be relocated and the costs of mothballing and maintaining a nonsalable piece of expensive real estate.

For many years, it has been popular to talk about the "fat" in the federal budget. The assumption is that much of the taxpayers' money is spent unnecessarily and could be eliminated without hurting anyone but a few hogs feeding at the public trough. Unfortunately, very few people can agree on which areas the unnecessary spending occurs. One person's waste is another's just due. But even where there is agreement, another consideration arises. When federal money is spent—whether wisely or unwisely—people become dependent on it. Should the spending be suddenly withdrawn, they find themselves without a livelihood in a world where livelihoods are becoming increasingly scarce. Of course, they can still vote and they are likely to vote against whoever cut off their source of income, regardless of justification. It is not a good time to be either a president or a member of Congress.

Under these circumstances, legislators are certain to search for "impersonal" means of handling the budget. The computer is the obvious answer. All it really does is to make computations on information that is fed into it. But when one of them is witnessed in operation, only the most sophisticated minds can retain a grasp of that fact. It creates the illusion of deliberation. It paints a picture of conscious choice between competing alternatives. I have noticed that people who operate them consistently—such as ticket agents in airline terminals—actually talk to their machines. A few days ago, a word processor in our office let out a loud squawk and a secretary said to me: "It is asking me whether it should hyphenate a word or go on to a new line."

What makes things really decisive, however, is that no one can argue with a computer. It is not going to change its "mind." (My son, who is a computer expert, has explained to me that it does not have a mind and that its "intelligence" is about on the level of an imbecile. Its asset is its fantastic memory and its prodigious capacity for work.) One can, of course, feed in a different set of assumptions and produce a new set of answers. But these will merely confuse the public, which is going to accept whatever seems to come from the most authoritative course.

To the computer should be added the influence of the political and governmental technician. This area has seen the most rapid political development in the history of the post–World War II era. Almost overnight has appeared a breed of technician who brings to the political game the techniques of computerization, polling, statistical surveys, and market analysis that have proved so successful in the business world. The campaign manager of forty or so years ago had a potbelly, chewed cigars, spoke with a soft Irish accent, and was on beautiful terms with all the ward leaders of every major city. The campaign manager of today is fashionably trim (he or she jogs every morning before breakfast), wears a three-piece suit, chews breath-a-mints, and would be inarticulate if the words "input," "output," "feedback," and "regressive analysis" were eliminated from the English language. He differs radically from his predecessors in one other respect. The old-timer cared nothing about politics as long as they brought in votes. The modern type insists on written policy positions that ultimately tend to find their way into government. Mated with the computer, this is a formidable force.

The executive branch of the government is already relying heavily on the computer. There is no doubt in my mind that the computer printouts of the Defense Department had an enormous influence on the policies that bogged us down in Vietnam. This is not surprising in view of the incredible complexity of the logistics. I see no prospect of this influence declining. If anything, it is going to become greater. Reagan's efforts to shrink the presence of the federal government have resulted in the shrinkage of federal aid programs. But the government itself remains deeply imbedded in our lives and is likely to become even more so.

This is not a prediction that the government will fall in the hands of computers. I do not see a world in which robots will drive us off the planet. But I do see a world in which computer operations open up new sources of power at the same time that older sources are declining. And this can create some subtle shifts in the composition of our government. Some of them have taken place already. The presidency is no longer the all-powerful force that it was under Johnson and Nixon. And Congress is no longer the complaisant rubber stamp for presidential foreign policy that it was during the extended era of the New Deal. There is a new relationship between the executive and the legislative branches of our government and I doubt that we will go back to the way it was before.

The president still has the power of the initiative. He can start balls rolling to which others must respond. In the field of foreign policy, this power is magnified. His control over the armed forces enables him to place American troops in a position where they must be rescued, and that can often be done only by a greater military commitment. Even here, however, there are a few straws in the wind that point to the possibilities of change. In the closing days of the Nixon administration, when there was widespread speculation that the president was becoming frantic under the pressures of Watergate, Secretary of Defense James R. Schlesinger asked the Joint Chiefs of Staff to notify him immediately if any of them received instructions from the White House to take military action. It was an extraordinary request. Obviously, Schlesinger wished to be in a position to throw up some kind of a roadblock in the event that the White House turned to military action as a diversion from scandal. (Incidentally, the law authorizes the president to bypass the Secretary of Defense and deal directly with the Joint Chiefs in regard to using the atomic bomb.) Ever since I heard the story, I have wondered what Schlesinger would, or could, have done. The mere fact that he was willing to try speaks volumes.

I have no blueprint for the future in mind, but certain forces that will determine that future have already emerged on the scene. One of the most important lies in the various fences that have been built to restrain the presidency. They are forces that very strong men can leap and no one can ever be certain that human beings will use legal authority that is in their hands. Just the same it is there. There are certain provisions under the Twenty-fifth Amendment to the Constitution whereby the vice-president can take over the government should the president become "crackers." The language is vague and lawyers have never succeeded in giving me a satisfactory construction of how it would work. That is not of any great importance. Should a moment of genuine emergency come along, no one would worry about legal niceties. They could await court determination after the whole thing was over, just as Abraham Lincoln suspended the writ of habeas corpus without causing any effective protest during the Civil War.

Nevertheless, what has been done so far is only fence building. The presidency has been subdued but not abolished, nor, in my judgment, will it become a mere figurehead post. The office is vital to the nation both as a unifying force and as the cutting edge of innovation. The circumstances that led the British kings to abdicate their managerial authority to prime ministers do not apply to us. But it is possible that under the new circumstances that are beginning to prevail many of the powers that were exercised only by the chief executive will be taken over by others. In this respect, Cabinet officers may assume far greater roles than they have played in the past. They have been mere servants of the president, and technically that remains their legal status. But the United States is remarkable in its capacity to change substance without changing forms. The Cabinet agencies have grown in size and complexity until it is no longer possible for the president to control all of them. This means that they will have more opportunity to act on their own—and sooner or later, men will be found to take advantage of that opportunity.

When I finished the *Twilight of the Presidency* in 1970, I was close to despair. I could see no end to the widening gulf between the president and the American people. Everything that I wrote then as a result of my observations remains valid: The presidency *is* a monarchy and the White House *is* a court. Now that I have been inside its walls, I can interpret the various revelations which emerge and it is clear to me that nothing there has changed. What *has* changed, however, is America. I had not taken into account the resiliency of our political and governmental system. What we have done, almost in terms of the Hegelian dialectic, is to build counterbalancing forces that are bringing us back to reality.

I am not happy with some of those counterbalances. Bureaucracy can be stultifying and I am wearied with political technicians who see the scene in terms of averages rather than men, women, and children. And I am terrified by the Gramm-Rudman approach to budgeting. No one lacking political accountability should be allowed to determine how taxpayers' money is spent. To all this, however, I comfort myself with a simple thought. As time goes on, counterbalances will be built to counterbalance the structures we have built to counterbalance the monarchical presidency. The system may lurch dangerously close to destruction. But in the long run it, like life, will continue.

Postscript

THE MANUSCRIPT OF this book had been completed and prepared for printing when the story of the clandestine arms shipment to Iran and transfer of funds to the Contras burst into the front pages. At the time this is being written, I have no idea of how it will develop. A wide variety of possibilities is obvious. It could be (although this is unlikely) that it will force President Reagan to resign from office. On the contrary, it is entirely possible (although again unlikely) that he will recapture the complete confidence of the nation and the whole issue will be relegated to the dustheap of history. More likely, he will limp along to the end of his term—still liked but no longer the unchallenged leader of the American polity.

For the purpose of this book, the outcome of the scandal does not matter except to historians and biographers of Mr. Reagan. Our interest lies in the impact of the events on the institution in the future. Enough has emerged already to give us some important clues. What counts here is not the extent to which some people may have broken the law. The overriding point is the evidence that they acted *in the president's name* but *without the president's express authority*. The essence of the affair—if the spokesmen are to be believed—is that the policy of the United States in the field of foreign affairs was made by anonymous functionaries who had no constitutional accountability to the people of this country. In short, the government was out of control.

Many of my friends refuse to believe that a Marine lieutenant colonel would take it upon himself to transfer millions of dollars of funds from arms sale to the Nicaraguan rebels. They think the president is lying when he says he knows nothing about it. However, I have a strong feeling that they find comfort in the thought that the whole thing is a fraud. They would rather have a president who is a liar than a president who cedes his constitutional role to subordinates. I can understand this viewpoint because my sense that the truth *is* being told leaves me in despair. It is depressing to think that our government is out of control.

Obviously, this could not have happened under a different president. The one I served kept a firm grip on every policy-making agency of the government. To my mind, however, that is irrelevant. I have been watching the growth of the White House Staff for many years. It has swollen to large proportions and has reached a size where several empires can be built within the walls of the Executive Mansion and the Executive Office building. Of these empires, the one that has become the most strongly entrenched is the National Security Council. In the creation of this group, presidents have fostered the growth of a monster that has superb opportunities for striking out on its own because it has only to deceive one man— the president himself. There are very few men and women who can resist the temptation to seize and exercise power when it is placed before them in such an alluring fashion. It was only a matter of time before some form of under-the-counter deal was arranged.

The National Security Council staff was originally formed to coordinate the advice of the relevant executive agencies so the president would be able to work out a coherent national policy. It was a good idea. It enabled the president to listen to adversary debate before making up his mind on security problems and, in a sense, it afforded some checks on the agencies so they would not operate on their own. Only a small staff was needed, as the real work was done in the State, Defense, Treasury, and Justice departments. Under President Kennedy, however, the staff began to grow and by the time Johnson reached the White House it included quite a number of technicians for the various areas of the world.

Under Nixon, the Council began to play the predominant role in foreign policy. Nixon's director of the Council was Henry Kissinger, who had answers for crises that no one else had ever considered. When a crisis would break out anywhere in the world, Nixon would call his Secretary of State, who would promise to get "my people" together and report back. The president would then call Kissinger, who would give him at least ten answers before hanging up the phone. Presidents like answers. It is simple to figure out how the Security Council post became elevated to the top of the heap. Kissinger himself was so aware of the potential power of the organization— power through its access to the president—that he was careful to keep it under control when he himself became Secretary of State.

To understand fully the attractions of the National Security Council staff to presidents, it is essential to examine one of the basic problems of the presidency— how the chief executive gets things done. Most Americans are under the illusion that he says "do it" and it happens. That picture is not altogether fallacious—but there are some complications. When he says "do it" to somebody who is directly dependent upon him, the response is prompt and complete. When he says it to an executive agency, however, the response is modified by bureaucratic machinery, which has an existence of its own. The reaction will be respectful, and if the White House sustains the pressure long enough it will produce the action desired. But the end result will not be achieved immediately. It comes as a climax to a long process in which paperwork must be duplicated and reduplicated; a wide ranging series of "bases" must be touched; and ingenious forms of sabotage will emerge if lower-level officials are displeased. This is the famous set of circumstances that led to French defeat during the Franco-Prussian War—the *"trahison des clercs."*

The agency heads, of course, would like to oblige the president as rapidly as possible. But they cannot prod the complicated organizations over which they preside beyond a certain point. For one thing, they are dealing with civil service regulations, which drastically limit their powers to hire and fire. For another thing, the bureaucratic machinery, for all its faults, is not totally without merit. Built into it are memory banks that will make someone aware of the fact that an idea that seemed bright, fresh, and sparkling to the president and his staff was actually an old chestnut that had been tried fifty years earlier and led to a disaster. There are values to such nitpicking scrutiny, and avoiding it altogether can be dangerous.

Nitpicking is not a very prominent characteristic of our presidents. They are usually strong, driving men who had to trample all over customary rules of procedures in order to attain their eminence. Had they played the political game by the regulations laid down by the Marquis of Queensbury, they would have remained bush leaguers. In some cases, they actually developed a contempt for orderly processes. Furthermore, they only have, at best, eight years in which to change history, and delays in the process are not welcomed. Consequently, a fine-tuned instrument that vibrates on their same wavelength and plunges into action immediately and effectively upon order appears to them as a blessing from the Almighty.

In practice, this has meant a National Security Council Staff that has given the president a capacity for direct action that he had never had before. Of course, much that it does must still involve the executive agencies, such as State, Defense, Justice, and Treasury. But there is a difference between the president dealing with them all by himself when he is plagued with other problems and having men and women who can devote all their time to exercising his authority to ride herd on a project. Furthermore, he can use the Council for important missions— such as MacFarlane's negotiations in Iran—without having to feed his ideas into the bureaucratic machinery. After all, the Council staff belongs to him. The executive agencies are subject to oversight by the Congress.

What this means is that we have established within the White House a group that can take far-ranging action and that is beholden to one man only. It is in a position to exercise his powers *even when he does now know that they are being exercised* and it is not subject to scrutiny by Congress unless the president himself approves the scrutiny. It can sit in on any meeting of government officials when the national security is the subject of discussion. But when it does so, it occupies a different kind of chair around the table from the others. The Secretary of State and the Secretary of Defense, for example, meet as equals hoping to come to an agreement before the president makes a final decision. The head of the National Security Council meets as the personal representative of the man who is going to do the deciding.

This is an instrument of potential power. The only ingredient that need be added to the Council to make it an active power is the presence in the White House of a president who is careless about details and somewhat unsure of his own abilities. Of course, the Council staff members cannot fly directly against his wishes; but as long as they can convince him that they are acting in accordance with his desires, they have wide latitude for their operations. The outcry over what happened in Iran and the transfer of money to the Contras in Nicaragua will probably ensure a period of strict conformance to constitutional standards. But the system that caused this deal is still intact and it is only a question of time until another set of circumstances arise that will tempt men and women to independent action.

Lew Deschler, the parliamentarian of the House of Representatives in the 1950's, taught me an important principle of law. It was that habit makes custom and custom makes law. The habit of reliance on the National Security Council is deeply engrained. How much longer will it be for the next steps to take place?

Of course, the Council involves only national security policy. But during the Lyndon Johnson regime, Joseph Califano began the construction of a staff to do for domestic policy what the NSC did in the international field. Thus far, his efforts have not borne the same fruit. Nevertheless, it was an idea that inspired considerable comment of a favorable nature and it seems to me inevitable that it will become a force. After all, the president has the same bureaucratic problems with such agencies as Labor, Agriculture, Education, Health and Welfare as he does with State, Defense, Justice and Treasury. If the spotlight should shift to the domestic field as the center of presidential concern, the NSC pattern would become very attractive.

Personally, I believe that the continued development of a personal presidential staff of considerable size is inevitable. I do not like it because it is another layer of insulation between the chief executive and the American people, but the complexity of our times leaves us little choice. The president needs some kind of machinery by which his programs and policies do not get lost in the bureaucratic maze. At the same time, however, we must not allow the virtues of the bureaucracy to be lost. It needs White House prodding—but only prodding. The departments must remain the "action arm" of the government because that is an arm that should be governed by rules of conduct.

There is no easy answer to this problem. To surround the White House staff with the same considerations that govern the agencies would raise serious constitutional questions. The doctrine of separation of powers is real and its values should not be lost. What we must do is to find some middle ground—some means that will give the president the advantages that come with a large staff but that will not allow it to run wild. That is a problem that should occupy our attention in the immediate future and perhaps some solutions will suggest themselves as the hearings on the Iranian operation run their course.

For our purposes, however, the important factor is the suggestion that presidential powers might be dispersed and actually exercised through people who are beholden to him but who have large areas of elbow room. What we have at the moment is a situation in which we are hoping that Howard Baker, as White House Chief of Staff, will fill that role. Could this be a foretaste of Parliamentary government? It can be brought about in a number of ways. The particular instance that we are examining here was one that was, at best, unfortunate. Nevertheless it indicates what could be done. Perhaps we are looking at the opening steps of a new presidential concept. Harry Truman kept over his desk a sign saying "The Buck Stops Here." In the future, it may well be that the sign will hang over a number of office doors behind which men and women will labor to solve problems. In the United Kingdom, all governmental actions are taken in the name of "Her Majesty's Government," even though she may have no knowledge of it until she picks up the *Times*. Could it be that we face an era in which all actions will be taken in the name of the "President of the United States" even though he (or she) may not know about it until the *Washington Post* is delivered to the White House in the morning?

Index